D0773281

SAVING ENDANGERED SPECIES
THE
RED WOLF
Help Save This Endangered Species!

Alison Imbriaco

MyReportLinks.com Books
an imprint of
Enslow Publishers, Inc. **E**
Box 398, 40 Industrial Road
Berkeley Heights, NJ 07922
USA

MyReportLinks.com Books, an imprint of Enslow Publishers, Inc. MyReportLinks® is a registered trademark of Enslow Publishers, Inc.

Copyright © 2008 by Enslow Publishers, Inc.

All rights reserved.

No part of this book may be reproduced by any means without the written permission of the publisher.

Library of Congress Cataloging-in-Publication Data

Imbriaco, Alison.
  The red wolf : help save this endangered species! / Alison Imbriaco.
      p. cm. — (Saving endangered species)
  Includes bibliographical references and index.
  ISBN-13: 978-1-59845-038-5
  ISBN-10: 1-59845-038-7
  1. Red wolf—Juvenile literature. 2. Endangered species—Juvenile literature. I. Title.
QL737.C22I43 2008
599.773—dc22
                                      2006020825
Printed in the United States of America

10 9 8 7 6 5 4 3 2 1

To Our Readers:
Through the purchase of this book, you and your library gain access to the Report Links that specifically back up this book.

The Publisher will provide access to the Report Links that back up this book and will keep these Report Links up to date on **www.myreportlinks.com** for five years from the book's first publication date.

We have done our best to make sure all Internet addresses in this book were active and appropriate when we went to press. However, the author and the Publisher have no control over, and assume no liability for, the material available on those Internet sites or on other Web sites they may link to.

The usage of the MyReportLinks.com Books Web site is subject to the terms and conditions stated on the Usage Policy Statement on **www.myreportlinks.com**.

A password may be required to access the Report Links that back up this book. The password is found on the bottom of page 4 of this book.

Any comments or suggestions can be sent by e-mail to comments@myreportlinks.com or to the address on the back cover.

Photo Credits: © Greg Koch, www.gkphotography.net, p. 1; © Lauren V. Greene, pp. 32, 44, 67, 73, 81, 96; ARKive, p. 36; Barron Crawford, USFWS, p. 10; Chattanooga Nature Center, p. 91; Curtis Carley, USFWS, p. 111; Defenders of Wildlife, pp. 69, 106; Ellen Marcus, USFWS, p. 18; Enslow Publishers, Inc., pp. 5, 92; Field Trip Earth, p. 34; International Wolf Center, p. 103; John and Karen Hollingsworth, USFWS, pp. 3, 41, 56; Library of Congress, pp. 16, 48, 50–51; Minnesota Department of Natural Resources, p. 20; MyReportLinks.com Books, p. 4; *National Geographic,* p. 39, National Wildlife, p. 59; Natural Worlds, p. 12; North Carolina Zoo, p. 108; Photos.com, pp. 21, 23; Point Defiance Zoo and Aquarium, p. 74; Red Wolf Recovery Project, USFWS, p. 54; Sacramento Zoo, p. 14; Scholastic, p. 89; Sewee Visitor and Environmental Education Center, USFWS, p. 53; Shutterstock, p. 46; The American Zoo and Aquarium Association, p. 94; The Nature Conservancy, p. 60; The Red Wolf Coalition, p. 65; The Red Wolf Sanctuary and Raptor Rehabilitation Center, p. 99; U.S. Fish and Wildlife Service (USFWS), pp. 5, 25, 62, 79, 83, 86, 109, 113; United States House of Representatives, p. 26; Virginia Living Museum, p. 29; Western North Carolina Nature Center, p. 31; Wild Canid Survival and Research Center, p. 97; Wildlife Science Center, p. 77; Wolf Haven International, p. 101; Wolf Park, p. 45.

Cover Photo: © Greg Koch, www.gkphotography.net

CONTENTS

MyReportLinks.com Books
Great Books, Great Links, Great for Research!

The Internet sites featured in this book can save you hours of research time. These Internet sites—we call them **"Report Links"**—are constantly changing, but we keep them up to date on our Web site.

When you see this "Approved Web Site" logo, you will know that we are directing you to a great Internet site that will help you with your research.

Give it a try! Type http://www.myreportlinks.com into your browser, click on the series title and enter the password, then click on the book title, and scroll down to the Report Links listed for this book.

The Report Links will bring you to great source documents, photographs, and illustrations. MyReportLinks.com Books save you time, feature Report Links that are kept up to date, and make report writing easier than ever! A complete listing of the Report Links can be found on pages 114–115 at the back of the book.

Please see "To Our Readers" on the copyright page for important information about this book, the MyReportLinks.com Web site, and the Report Links that back up this book.

Please enter **SRW1825** if asked for a password.

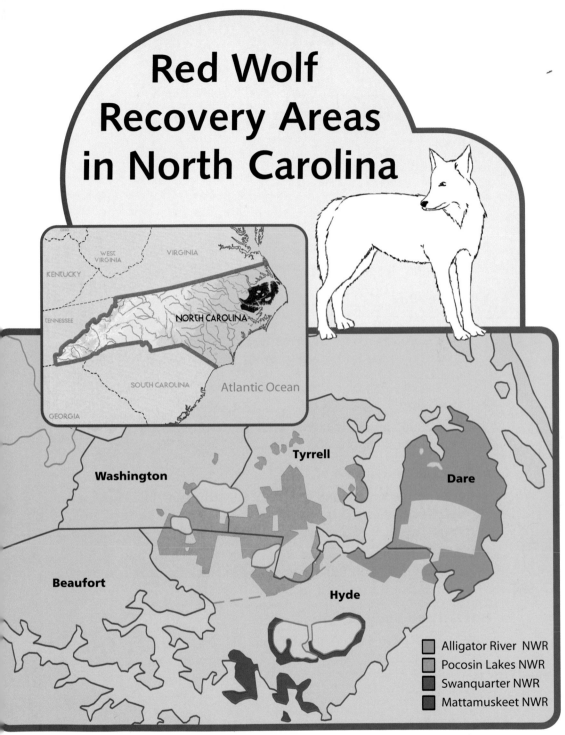

Red Wolf Recovery Areas in North Carolina

WEST VIRGINIA

VIRGINIA

KENTUCKY

TENNESSEE

NORTH CAROLINA

SOUTH CAROLINA

Atlantic Ocean

GEORGIA

Washington

Tyrrell

Dare

Beaufort

Hyde

Alligator River NWR
Pocosin Lakes NWR
Swanquarter NWR
Mattamuskeet NWR

Map adapted from the U.S. Fish and Wildlife Service Red Wolf Recovery Program

▲ *As of 2006, the wild red wolf population numbered about 100 wolves in 17 packs ranging across 1.7 million acres of private and public lands in the five North Carolina counties represented on this map. The Alligator River and Pocosin Lakes National Wildlife Refuges are the major public lands used for red wolf recovery.*

RED WOLF FACTS

▶ **Kingdom**

Animalia (animal)

▶ **Order**

Carnivore

▶ **Family**

Canidae (canids)

▶ **Scientific Name**

Canis rufus, from Latin *canis,* "dog," and *rufus,* "red"

▶ **Distribution**

Wild red wolves live on more than 1.7 million acres in eastern North Carolina. A few wolves live on several small islands. Thirty-eight zoos and other facilities provide space for captive wolves.

▶ **Population**

As of 2006, more than 100 wild red wolves lived in North Carolina, while about 200 wolves lived in captivity.

▶ **Physical Description**

Fur is mostly brown and buff colored with some black on the back. Sometimes the fur behind the ears, on the muzzle, and toward the back of the legs is reddish.

White markings extend up long, narrow muzzles and inside large, pointed ears. Tail tips are usually black. Most red wolves have reddish fur on their heads.

▶ **Head and Body Length**

55 to 65 inches (140 to 165 centimeters), or about 4 feet (1 meter)

▶ **Average Shoulder Height**

26 inches (67 centimeters)

▶ **Weight**

The average female weighs 52 pounds (24 kilograms); the average male weighs 61 pounds (28 kilograms).

▶ Diet/Prey

White-tailed deer, raccoons, rabbits, mice, opossums, and nutria

▶ Size at Birth

Less than 1 pound (.45 kilogram)

▶ Litter Size

Usually two to six pups. Pups are born in April and May.

▶ Habitat

Forests, marshes, and agricultural lands. Wolves are habitat generalists and can thrive in most settings where there is sufficient prey and few people.

▶ Life Span

About half of the pups born in the wild die soon after they are born. Wolves that survive their first year live an average of seven years.

▶ Threats

Hybridization, loss of habitat, vehicles, disease, hunting

Part of our heritage is our nation's war against the wolf . . . Never before has one species declared such total war on a fellow species.

Rick McIntyre, *War Against the Wolf*

Chapter 1 ▶

THE LAST WOLVES

He moves through the tangled underbrush with the tireless trot of his kind. Large front paws and long, thin legs help him pass quietly through the briars and weeds of the marshland vegetation. In the distance, large machines move steadily up and down, pumping oil from below the earth, and large refineries process the oil. Not so far away is the city of Galveston, Texas.

Cattle graze in nearby pastures. On another day he might wait to see if a calf strays from the herd. A calf would make an excellent dinner, and food has not been easy to find.

He is not well. Parasites drain his energy. Mange mites have eaten away some of his tan fur, leaving patches of skin exposed to sun and rain. Hookworms living in his intestines make it difficult to digest the food he can find.

He hears a mouse scurry through the weeds. He is hungry, and the mouse would be a tasty snack, but he does not stop to pounce on it. He is looking for something else.

▲ *Thanks to the efforts of government wildlife officials, zoos, and groups of concerned citizens, there are now about one hundred red wolves in the wild and two hundred in captivity.*

Although he is hungry and sick, he will not stop. He is looking for another of his kind. Suddenly, he sees another animal. It is like him—but not exactly like him. He stops to look and then advances, wagging his tail, but the animal runs away. The red wolf stands still, confused and lonely.

He cannot know that he is the last wild red wolf. Soon he will be trapped by men who want to help him. He will be taken to another climate, and he will be given medicine to get rid of the parasites. He will find a mate, and he will help to raise pups. But he will never again be wild.

Although this sounds like a work of fiction, it is a true story. In 1980, there were so few red wolves remaining in the United States that wildlife experts determined the only way to save them was to capture them, breed them, and try to release some back to the wild. While that program has been successful, the struggle to save the species is far from over.

▶ The First Wolves

Wolves began to separate from other mammals about 55 million years ago, when a mammal species developed specialized teeth for eating prey.[1] These teeth, called carnassials, are behind the long canine teeth, on the sides of the animal's mouth. They function like scissors, cutting flesh and tissue into bite-sized pieces.

Over many millions of years, the first mammal with carnassial teeth evolved into a wide range of meat eaters including cats, weasels, raccoons, and bears. Cats became a separate species almost 40 million years ago. About 30 million years ago, the ancestors of the dog family, canids, separated from the ancestors of bears and raccoons. Foxes and wolves began to develop separately about 15 million years ago.

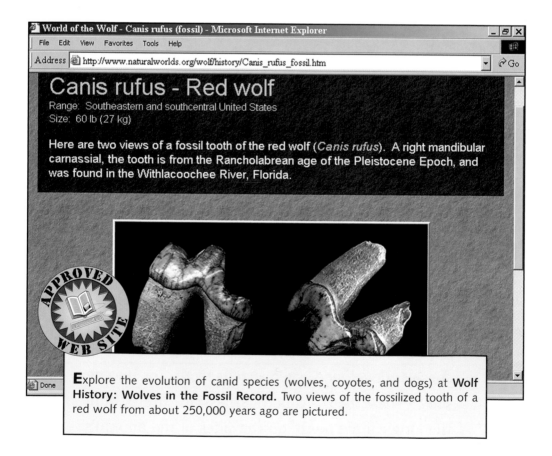

World of the Wolf - Canis rufus (fossil) - Microsoft Internet Explorer

File   Edit   View   Favorites   Tools   Help

Address http://www.naturalworlds.org/wolf/history/Canis_rufus_fossil.htm   Go

Canis rufus - Red wolf

Range: Southeastern and southcentral United States
Size: 60 lb (27 kg)

Here are two views of a fossil tooth of the red wolf (*Canis rufus*). A right mandibular carnassial, the tooth is from the Rancholabrean age of the Pleistocene Epoch, and was found in the Withlacoochee River, Florida.

Done

Explore the evolution of canid species (wolves, coyotes, and dogs) at **Wolf History: Wolves in the Fossil Record.** Two views of the fossilized tooth of a red wolf from about 250,000 years ago are pictured.

Most scientists agree that the wolf family began in North America when animals similar to modern coyotes grew larger, with longer legs and stronger jaws. These new carnivores walked on their toes instead of walking flat-footed as cats and bears do.[2] By about one million years ago, wolves probably looked much like modern red wolves do.[3]

Some wolves moved north, growing still larger. Another branch of the wolf family migrated to South America to become the dire wolf, which had much larger teeth and a large head. The dire wolf, like many other wolf species, is extinct.

Between six hundred thousand and three hundred thousand years ago, wolves crossed the land bridge that once connected North America and Asia and migrated throughout Asia and Europe.[4] Many thousands of years ago, the gray wolf migrated back from Asia to North America.

▶ Wolves and People

In Asia and Europe, humans came to hate wolves because both competed for the same prey. Eventually, people began to domesticate sheep and goats for their own use. Since killing domestic animals was easier than killing wild prey, wolves sometimes killed farm animals (although wild red wolves prefer wild game to domestic animals). As people settled on land and cut down

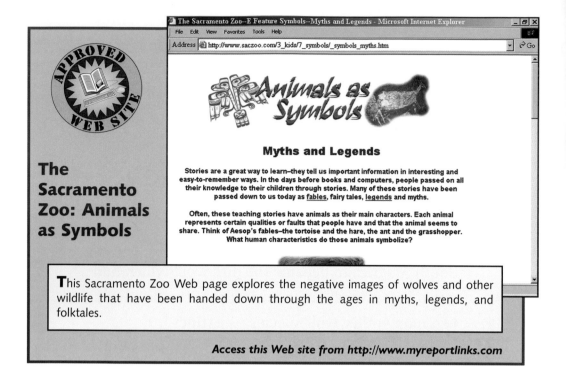

The Sacramento Zoo--E Feature Symbols--Myths and Legends - Microsoft Internet Explorer

File   Edit   View   Favorites   Tools   Help

Address http://www.saczoo.com/3_kids/7_symbols/_symbols_myths.htm   Go

Animals as Symbols

Myths and Legends

Stories are a great way to learn—they tell us important information in interesting and easy-to-remember ways. In the days before books and computers, people passed on all their knowledge to their children through stories. Many of these stories have been passed down to us today as <u>fables</u>, fairy tales, <u>legends</u> and myths.

Often, these teaching stories have animals as their main characters. Each animal represents certain qualities or faults that people have and that the animal seems to share. Think of Aesop's fables—the tortoise and the hare, the ant and the grasshopper. What human characteristics do those animals symbolize?

The Sacramento Zoo: Animals as Symbols

This Sacramento Zoo Web page explores the negative images of wolves and other wildlife that have been handed down through the ages in myths, legends, and folktales.

Access this Web site from http://www.myreportlinks.com

trees for farmland and fuel, they pushed the wolves into smaller and smaller areas. Contact between wolves and domestic animals, and between wolves and people, increased.

Some wolves were domesticated by humans and became dogs. Evidence suggests that twelve thousand years ago, people in the Middle East had dogs, indicating that some wolves became domestic animals long before sheep and goats did.[5] Even so, humans' hatred and fear of wild wolves grew.

People killed in wars were left lying on the ground, and wolves sometimes ate the dead bodies, horrifying those who saw it. During the Middle Ages, many people died from the plague, a disease that spread quickly, which provided wolves with more dead human bodies. Hatred of wolves grew stronger.

The way that some wolves kill their prey also disturbs people. Wolves hunt in packs, jumping at an animal and tearing at its flesh as it runs, ripping it apart while the animal is still conscious. To many people, this method of devouring prey seems horrible. To those wolves, this is the only way they know to survive. Red wolves, however, eat smaller prey than other wolves, so most of their hunting is thought to be done by individual wolves or a pair.

Fairy tales and other children's stories often portray wolves as menacing creatures, so children reading those tales became afraid of wolves. Fear of wolves led to folklore about werewolves (people who become wolves), and some thought wolves were in league with the devil.

▶ Killing Wolves in North America

Over time, people hunted and killed many kinds of animals for their meat or fur, but people killed wolves because they hated and feared them. By the time Europeans arrived in North America, wolves had almost disappeared from settled areas of Europe. Although many of the earliest settlers in the American colonies had never seen a real

FRANK LESLIE'S Boy's & Girl's Weekly,

An Illustrated Journal of Amusement, Adventure, and Instruction.

Vol. 1.—No. 18.   NEW YORK, MARCH 2, 1867.   Five Cents a Copy. $2.50 Yearly.

DEADLY ATTACK OF A WOLF ON A MAN.

There is a common belief that only wild beasts of the largest and savagest kind will voluntarily attack man, except when they are in large droves. There was, however, in 1859, an instance in which a wolf attacked a farmer who was chopping wood near Lexington, Sanilac County, Michigan, and with such ferocity that, despite his utmost exertions, he was overmastered by the furious animal. It appears that early one morning the unfortunate settler was engaged in lopping some branches at a short distance from his cottage, when a wolf started from a thicket, and before the farmer could defend himself, grasped his throat with such deadly power that he dropped his ax.

His cries brought his wife to the door of the cottage; seeing the danger of her husband, the noble woman, with all that scorn of danger which distinguishes her sex when those she loves are in danger, ran to the spot, and, seizing the ax, struck the wolf so well-aimed a blow, that it compelled him to release the man.

Nothing daunted, the brave woman faced the furious beast with such coolness and courage that, after a short struggle, the wolf lay dead at her feet.

The woman then turned to her husband, and vainly endeavored to stop the blood which gushed from his throat. It was all in vain, for the unhappy man breathed his last in her arms.

On examination it was found that the fangs of the monster had as completely severed his windpipe as though the throat had been cut with a razor.

RECOLLECTIONS OF MY SCHOOL-DAYS AT MAPLETON HALL.

CHAPTER V.—HOME FOR THE HOLIDAYS.

The half-year term at Mapleton Hall ended with Christmas-tide. The last Friday before Christmas was always examination-day. The clergy and other professional men of the town and country attended in great ceremony. Many of the pupils' parents came into the town the day before and filled the Mapleton Tavern to overflowing.

The next afternoon they went away, taking their sons with them. During their stay the town was all bustle and excitement. The boys at the school had full liberty to visit their friends, and many were the happy greetings of father and son, mother and child, sister and brother.

The evening before examination-day Mrs. Milner gave a reception to the pupils and their friends. This entertainment commenced quite early in the evening, and before midnight her halls were deserted.

Frank and I expected no friends, and for that reason perhaps tried to look upon the affair with indifference. But when we heard that there was to be music and quadrilles, we relented a little. Then came the magic word "supper!"

"I ain't much of a ladies' man," said Frank, with all the indifference of a man of the world; "so it won't be worse than tooth-pulling to me to be without a partner; but when a young fellow with a healthy appetite like mine thinks of snubbing sponge-cake and sweetmeats, to say nothing of lemonade, that's what I call carrying the war into Africa. Don't you think, Wesley, we had better drop in about supper-time?"

DEADLY ATTACK OF A WOLF UPON A MAN, AND HEROIC CONDUCT OF THE MAN'S WIFE.

▲ *European settlers to North America brought their fear and hatred of wolves with them. This weekly newspaper from 1867 features the story of a "deadly attack" by a wolf on a man in frontier Michigan in 1859. An illustration shows the man's wife wielding an axe to save her husband. In reality, wolves had more to fear from humans than humans did from wolves.*

wolf, fear and hatred of wolves was part of their culture.

Biologists think that red wolves once hunted in forested lands from Pennsylvania to Florida and from the East Coast to central Texas. Red wolves may even have lived as far north as Ontario, Canada.[6] As soon as the first settlers arrived along the eastern shores of North America, they set about ridding the land of wolves. One of the first laws passed in the colony of Virginia provided a bounty, or reward, for anyone who killed a wolf and brought its head to the colony's commander.[7] As settlers moved west, so did wolf bounties, as bounty hunters killed thousands of wolves.

Wolves lost their habitat as people cut down forests to make farmland. Over time, the remaining wolves were shot, trapped, and poisoned, with nowhere to go. Eventually, wolves began to disappear from the lower forty-eight states.

▶ Early Research

By the time anyone became interested in wolves from a scientific point of view, there were few wolves left to study. In 1791, John Bartram, the first scientist to describe red wolves, believed they were a subspecies of the gray wolf. In 1851, naturalists John James Audubon and John Bachman declared that three species of wolf lived in North America: "the gray wolf in the north, the

Gray wolf............80–120 lbs.
Red wolf.............45–80 lbs.
Coyote................20–45 lbs.
Red fox...............10–15 lbs.

Ellen Marcus, USFWS

▲ This illustration from the United States Fish and Wildlife Service shows the comparative sizes of the gray wolf, red wolf, coyote, and red fox.

black wolf in Florida and the Southeast, and a red wolf in Texas and Arkansas." Eventually the Florida wolf was named *Canis ater,* and the Texas wolf was named *Canis rufus.* In 1937, another scientist classified the Florida wolves and red wolves as a single species, *Canis rufus.*[8]

Part of the difficulty in identifying and naming red wolves, aside from the fact that they had almost disappeared before anyone tried, is that red wolves are not really red, and the black wolves of Florida were probably not really black. Red wolves usually have light brown fur, although the color of their coats ranges from tan to black. They usually have reddish fur on their faces, ears, and legs.

Red Wolf: Species, Subspecies, or Hybrid?

Scientists do not even agree that *Canis rufus* is a distinct species. Some have argued that the red wolf is a subspecies of the gray wolf. David Mech (pronounced *meech*), a scientist with the United States Geological Survey and an expert on wolves, suggests that red wolves are a cross between gray wolves and coyotes, the result of interbreeding between those species.[9] An important voice on behalf of the red wolf is Ronald Nowak, who was endangered species coordinator for the United States Fish and Wildlife Service (often shortened to Fish and Wildlife, or FWS) until he resigned in 1997. Nowak has concluded that red wolves are directly descended from the original North American wolf.[10]

Extinct in the Wild

Nowak's conclusion was especially important because in the fall of 1973, FWS had just begun to develop a red wolf recovery plan. The Endangered Species Act of 1973 became law in December of that year, and since it only protects "true" species and not hybrids, it was important that red wolves were considered a distinct species.

By 1973, biologists realized that red wolves had become so few in number that they could not find enough mates in their own species. At the same time, coyotes, which had once lived only in

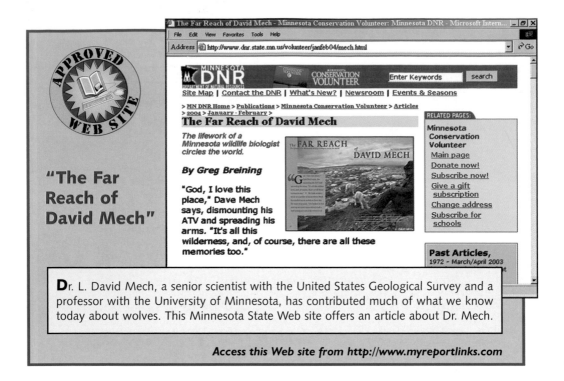

APPROVED WEB SITE

"The Far Reach of David Mech"

The Far Reach of David Mech - Minnesota Conservation Volunteer: Minnesota DNR - Microsoft Intern...

File   Edit   View   Favorites   Tools   Help

Address http://www.dnr.state.mn.us/volunteer/janfeb04/mech.html   Go

MINNESOTA **DNR**   CONSERVATION VOLUNTEER   Enter Keywords   search

Site Map | Contact the DNR | What's New? | Newsroom | Events & Seasons

> MN DNR Home > Publications > Minnesota Conservation Volunteer > Articles
> 2004 > January - February >

The Far Reach of David Mech

The lifework of a Minnesota wildlife biologist circles the world.

THE FAR REACH of DAVID MECH

By Greg Breining

"G

"God, I love this place," Dave Mech says, dismounting his ATV and spreading his arms. "It's all this wilderness, and, of course, there are all these memories too."

RELATED PAGES:

Minnesota Conservation Volunteer
Main page
Donate now!
Subscribe now!
Give a gift subscription
Change address
Subscribe for schools

Past Articles,
1972 - March/April 2003

Dr. L. David Mech, a senior scientist with the United States Geological Survey and a professor with the University of Minnesota, has contributed much of what we know today about wolves. This Minnesota State Web site offers an article about Dr. Mech.

Access this Web site from http://www.myreportlinks.com

the West, were moving east into areas where red wolves lived. Generally, wolves and coyotes do not live together, but the last red wolves, unable to find mates of their own species, were mating with coyotes and raising hybrid pups.

Biologists became convinced that red wolves would become extinct if left in the wild. In 1974, conservationists working with the FWS Red Wolf Recovery Team began to trap wolves and hybrids. They sent the animals they believed to be wolves to a facility made available by the Point Defiance Zoo in Tacoma, Washington. The biologists killed the wolflike animals they believed to be hybrids. In 1980 near Galveston, Texas, the recovery team

▲ *It is easy to see how a red wolf–coyote hybrid would be difficult to distinguish from a red wolf. This red wolf has markings similar to those of the coyote pictured on page 23.*

trapped what was thought to be the last wild red wolf. That capture meant red wolves were then considered extinct in the wild.

Recovery

As the captive red wolves mated and had pups in their new home in Washington, scientists saw that some of the offspring were actually hybrids. They eliminated the hybrids from the breeding program and were eventually left with only fourteen true red wolves. Those fourteen would serve as the founders of all red wolf generations to come.

In 1987, the FWS Red Wolf Recovery Team began releasing red wolves in the marshy and forested land of the Alligator River National Wildlife Refuge in North Carolina. Over the years, the red wolves' territory expanded. It now comprises more than one million acres, including three wildlife refuges and privately owned land. By 2006, more than one hundred wolves lived in the wild. Unfortunately, coyotes also moved into the area during the 1990s, so by 2002, there were at least seventeen hybrid wolf-coyotes in the wolves' territory.[11]

Threats to Recovery

According to the IUCN-World Conservation Union, the world's largest conservation network, the greatest threat to the red wolf is hybridization.[12]

▲ *Coyotes are smaller than red wolves and have a narrower head. Deforestation in parts of the coyote's western habitat forced coyotes east, where red wolves, already low in number, began mating with them.*

Scientists are still trying to find ways to prevent wolves and coyotes from crossbreeding in the wild. At the same time, zoos around the country provide space for wolves to breed in captivity. Through captive breeding, scientists can preserve the wolves' gene pool.

Money, or lack of it, affects the red wolf's ability to recover, however. The Red Wolf Recovery Program can continue to be funded only if people continue to believe it is important to save red wolves and other endangered species. Captive breeding also requires money. Zoos can provide homes for captive wolves only if the zoos can afford to provide the space.

Public attitudes also affect recovery efforts. For thousands of years, people have feared wolves. Some of that fear lingers today, making it difficult to find space where wolves can roam free.

▶ The ESA Under Attack

Now, the greatest threat to the red wolf and every other endangered species in the United States is an attack on the Endangered Species Act itself. A bill passed by the House of Representatives in 2005, H.R. 2384, would help weaken the act by making it easier for developers to build by removing protections for critical habitat. Critical habitat is land determined to be necessary for a species' survival. If a similar bill also introduced in the Senate

U.S. Fish & Wildlife Service

Kid's Corner

Endangered Means There Is Still Time
Species Spotlight | How Can Kids Help? | Educators
Learn More | Endangered Species Program

Endangered Means There is Still Time

USFWS
Endangered
Species
Program
Kid's Corner

APPROVED
WEB SITE

On this page for kids, the United States Fish and Wildlife Service (USFWS), which is responsible for protecting endangered species, offers ways in which you can become involved in saving those species and our environment.

Access this Web site from http://www.myreportlinks.com

in 2005 is passed, it will be combined with the bill already passed in the House. Without the strong protections of the Endangered Species Act, species such as the red wolf, bald eagle, whooping crane, and others threatened with extinction would not have survived this long.

What You Can Do to Help Save Red Wolves

The first step toward helping an endangered species is learning about it. You are already taking that step by reading this book. You can learn more by following the links in this book to Web sites that offer reliable information about red wolves

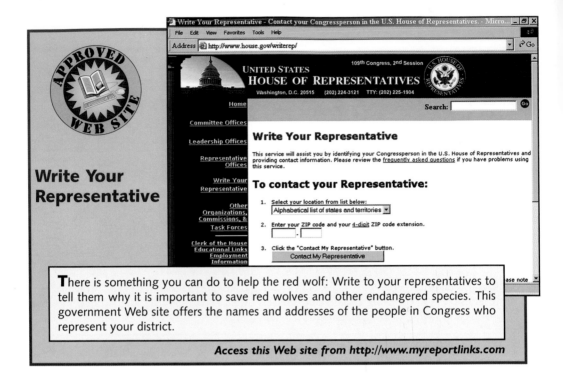

Write Your Representative

There is something you can do to help the red wolf: Write to your representatives to tell them why it is important to save red wolves and other endangered species. This government Web site offers the names and addresses of the people in Congress who represent your district.

Access this Web site from http://www.myreportlinks.com

and their habitat. As you learn about red wolves, share what you learn with the people around you. Let them know about the current threats to the Endangered Species Act and the consequences for endangered wildlife if the act is weakened.

You can also visit a wildlife refuge in your area to learn about the species it protects. Then write to your congressional representatives to tell them how important wildlife refuges are to you.

Visit the zoo closest to you and ask about red wolves. Even if the zoo does not have red wolves, it may participate in the captive-breeding program. If it does not, find out why. Perhaps the zoo in your area does not think there is public support for red wolf recovery. You might help raise public support by talking to people about the program. You might even write a letter to the editor of your local paper to inform others about the need for a red wolf captive-breeding program. If your class or your school participates in fund-raising projects, find out about programs that allow people to "adopt" a red wolf.

One roadblock to red wolf recovery is the species' negative image. You can help change that negative image by stating the facts: that wolves will run away from humans rather than attack them, and that wolves can be beneficial to farmers by controlling the numbers of deer, raccoons, and mice on farmers' lands.

There are other creative ways to help the environment and endangered species. To find ideas, visit Aza's Web, a Web site of the American Zoo and Aquarium Association. This Web site describes what young people can do—and are doing—to help endangered species. You really can make a difference in whether a species survives or not.

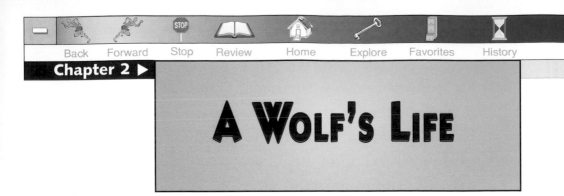

A WOLF'S LIFE

Among a red wolf's first impressions of the world is the feeling of soft, wiggly bodies providing warmth and companionship. Wolf pups are born blind and deaf, and they weigh less than a pound.[1] Too small to stay warm by themselves, they squirm into a pile with their brothers and sisters to survive while their mother is away. As they huddle together for warmth, the pups learn an important lesson about being wolves: They are social animals, and they need to know how to live with other wolves.

In the spring, females usually give birth to two to six pups, although a litter may occasionally be as small as one pup or as large as eight or more.[2] Before giving birth, the mothers locate dens in hollow trees or under rock outcroppings. Sometimes the mothers and fathers work together to dig into ditch banks or under piles of brush to make their dens. Wolf parents sometimes also dig more than one den so they can move the puppies to a new home as they grow.

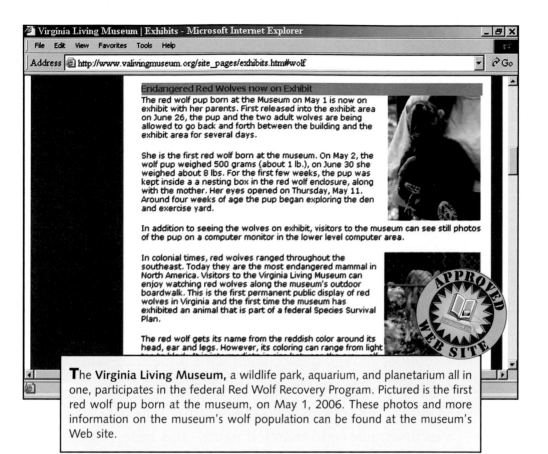

Virginia Living Museum | Exhibits - Microsoft Internet Explorer

File   Edit   View   Favorites   Tools   Help

Address http://www.valivingmuseum.org/site_pages/exhibits.htm#wolf   Go

Endangered Red Wolves now on Exhibit

The red wolf pup born at the Museum on May 1 is now on exhibit with her parents. First released into the exhibit area on June 26, the pup and the two adult wolves are being allowed to go back and forth between the building and the exhibit area for several days.

She is the first red wolf born at the museum. On May 2, the wolf pup weighed 500 grams (about 1 lb.), on June 30 she weighed about 8 lbs. For the first few weeks, the pup was kept inside a a nesting box in the red wolf enclosure, along with the mother. Her eyes opened on Thursday, May 11. Around four weeks of age the pup began exploring the den and exercise yard.

In addition to seeing the wolves on exhibit, visitors to the museum can see still photos of the pup on a computer monitor in the lower level computer area.

In colonial times, red wolves ranged throughout the southeast. Today they are the most endangered mammal in North America. Visitors to the Virginia Living Museum can enjoy watching red wolves along the museum's outdoor boardwalk. This is the first permanent public display of red wolves in Virginia and the first time the museum has exhibited an animal that is part of a federal Species Survival Plan.

The red wolf gets its name from the reddish color around its head, ear and legs. However, its coloring can range from light

APPROVED WEB SITE

The **Virginia Living Museum,** a wildlife park, aquarium, and planetarium all in one, participates in the federal Red Wolf Recovery Program. Pictured is the first red wolf pup born at the museum, on May 1, 2006. These photos and more information on the museum's wolf population can be found at the museum's Web site.

▶ Infancy

Females give birth in April or May. The newborn pups bear little resemblance to adult wolves. Their eyes are closed, their ears are pressed close to their heads, and their heads are round instead of long and narrow like an adult wolf's head. Their fur color, which is usually very gray, also differs from their parents' fur color. Within about ten days, their ears pop up, although they are floppy for another month or so. A few days later, their dark-blue eyes open.[3] However, another week or two will pass before the puppies hear and see very well.

The puppies grow fast during their first weeks. After about a month, they are strong enough to wander out of the den to play close to the entrance. They are not allowed to wander far.

One nature writer watched a gray wolf mother teaching her pups to stay put while she was gone. She left her pups and set off to hunt for food. As soon as she was out of sight, she stopped and lay low. An adventurous pup had followed her and suddenly found itself face to face with its mother. She barked, and the pup "stopped short, looked about as though preoccupied with something else, then . . . began to edge back the way he had come." The mother accompanied the pup back to its littermates and then left again. This time, none of the pups followed her.[4]

▶ Dominance

As the pups grow, they play and wrestle with one another and with older wolves in their family. They learn to use their muscles, and they practice skills they will use later as hunters. They also begin to learn about dominance.

Wolves live in family groups called packs. Red wolf packs usually include parents, their offspring from the previous year, and new pups. The pups need to learn the social rules of the pack.

This young wolf pup is featured on **Animal Facts: Red Wolf,** a Web page of the Western North Carolina Nature Center, which is part of the captive-breeding program designed to release red wolves into the wild.

Each pack has a dominance hierarchy, a social organization in which each individual has a rank, or place, in the group. The wolves at the top are the alpha wolves. Each pack has an alpha male and an alpha female. The other wolves are submissive to the alpha wolves but some may be dominant compared to other wolves in the pack. Each wolf has a specific rank in the social order, although the order may change over time as different wolves assert themselves. If only two wolves travel with an alpha wolf, those two wolves will need to establish which of them is more dominant and which is submissive.

Friendship

Dominance and submission are basic to wolf behavior. At the same time, the wolf pups that wiggle close and play together form strong social bonds that will probably last throughout their lives. A naturalist who spent many years observing wolves noted, "The strongest impression remaining with me after watching the wolves . . . was their friendliness."[5]

▲ These red wolf pups snuggle in their den on a farm in North Carolina. Lauren Greene, program director of the Red Wolf Coalition at the time, took this photograph while accompanying members of the Red Wolf Recovery Team. Recovery depends upon the cooperation of private landowners, since, as Ms. Greene points out, "You can't tell the wolves they can only live on the national wildlife refuges in the area."

Based on his observations, David Mech, who studied gray wolves for many years, concluded that wolves make friendly gestures toward one another simply to get a friendly response. They want to know that other wolves like them.[6]

Wolf pups form strong bonds with their family members during their first months. At the age of about three months, pups seem to lose the ability to form strong social bonds. They remain emotionally attached to their pack, but they become afraid of strangers.[7]

Pack Rules

Within the pack, the alpha wolves have privileges. They probably get the first choice of meat when a hunt is successful. They also have responsibilities. They often lead the others during a hunt, and they are responsible for defending the territory.

However, government within a pack does not seem to require blind following of the leader. Observers have noted that, while the alpha wolf is in charge, other wolves seem to express opinions and have certain rights, especially regarding food.

Pack organization also allows for fun. Adult wolves play with each other as well as with the puppies. Wolves sometimes hide and then jump out in front of another wolf, and they play tag. Sometimes they bring things, such as pieces of food, to another wolf, or they may pick up a stick and pretend they hold something special.[8]

▶ Feeding a Growing Family

For the first month of their lives, wolf pups depend on their mother's milk for nourishment. Then the father and older brothers and sisters begin to help with feeding the puppies. They do this by regurgitating, or bringing up, partially digested food from their own stomachs. When a wolf brings food for pups, it squeaks to call them. The pups then run to it and beg by licking and

Field Trip Earth - Microsoft Internet Explorer

File   Edit   View   Favorites   Tools   Help

Address http://www.fieldtripearth.org/media_image.xml?object_id=1871&file_id=4394   Go

Red Wolf Puppies at Four Weeks
Photo courtesy Chris Lasher, North Carolina Zoological Park

Go Back

View Related Media

Field Trip Earth Home

These four-week-old red wolf pups were photographed at the North Carolina Zoological Park. On the **Field Trip Earth: Red Wolves of Alligator River** Web site, you can learn about the physical differences between wolves and coyotes, wolf packs and pack behavior, and more.

pushing at the older wolf's mouth or putting their little mouths around the larger wolf's mouth. In response, the adult wolf brings up a pile of semi-liquid food.

The begging behavior of pups becomes part of adult wolves' "vocabulary." David Mech described a "group ceremony" that seems to be a way of expressing affection. In this ceremony, pack members gather around the leader and behave like pups begging for food as they push their muzzles against the leader's muzzle, lick the leader's face, or put their mouths gently around the leader's mouth. This group ceremony seems to take place without any apparent reason, but it often happens when the pack comes together after being separated.[9]

Pack members do more than help feed wolf puppies. Older brothers and sisters sometimes babysit while the mother hunts for food. As the puppies spend more time outside the den, adults play with them. In fact, both male and female wolves seem to want to care for puppies, whether or not the puppies are their own.

Teeth

When wolf puppies are about four months old, they begin to lose their puppy teeth and grow adult teeth. Like other members of the *Canidae*

ARKive, an online database featuring still and moving images of endangered species, features this image of red wolf pups. On the **ARKive: Red Wolf** (*Canis rufus*) pages, you can view more images of red wolves.

(dog) family, wolves have forty-two teeth, and these teeth are essential for their survival.

The largest teeth are the four canine teeth, which wolves use to attack and grab prey. Canines can be more than two inches (five centimeters) long, including the part in the gums.[10] The twelve front teeth are sharp incisor teeth that wolves use to cut meat away from their prey. Behind the canines are premolars and molars. The last premolar and first molar teeth, about halfway along both sides of a wolf's mouth, are called carnassial teeth.

These teeth are especially effective at cutting away chunks of meat and muscle to swallow. The molars at the back of wolves' mouths can crush bones so that wolves can eat the bone marrow. Wolves' teeth are not designed for chewing, however. Wolves gulp down large chunks of meat.

Supporting the teeth are strong jaws and muscles so that wolves can disable and kill large animals. No domestic dog can match the biting power of wolves. Wolves' long skulls are a result of the need for strong jaws and use of all the teeth for cutting meat and crushing bone to bits.

Wolf Senses

Wolves need an acute sense of smell, excellent hearing, and sharp eyesight to survive as hunters. Their ability to detect smells may be one hundred times greater than that of humans. Because they use their sense of smell when they hunt, wolves hunt "into" the wind or breeze, which means they feel the air moving on their faces. The moving air carries scents to the wolves, but it carries the scent of wolves away from animals in front of them.

Red wolves' ears stand about four inches (ten centimeters) above their heads, and muscles allow wolves to turn their ears independently to catch sounds. Wolves hear more than humans hear, and they are especially good at hearing high-pitched sounds. Tests indicate that wolves can hear clearly in the very high range where bats make sounds.[11]

Wolves also see well, although they see differently than people see. While wolves probably see better when there is less light, their eyes do not include a fovea, the part of the human eye that is especially good at seeing details.[12] Still, wolves can see movement at great distances.

▶ Fur

As wolf pups grow strong and start to develop keen senses, they begin to look more like adults. At the age of two or three months, adult fur begins to replace puppy fur. Longer guard hairs provide the color, which can range from tan to almost black. An under layer of shorter, denser fur traps air and provides insulation. Periodically, wolves shed their fur and grow new fur.

Besides protecting wolves from rain and cold temperatures, their fur, including the lighter and darker patterns on their faces, helps them communicate. For example, wolves, coyotes, and many dogs have hairs on the back of their necks and shoulders that stand up when they are angry. Lighter hairs around wolves' mouths and ears help to emphasize facial expressions, which scientists are just beginning to understand. In addition, wolves' eyes and lips are often outlined in black to make them more noticeable.

▶ Communication

Wolves communicate with one another in many ways. Often, dominant wolves assert their position simply by staring at other wolves. Submissive wolves may narrow their eyes to slits and pull the corners of their mouths back. Wolves also use their tails to communicate, which is why the tip of the tail is often darker to help emphasize its position. When wolves are relaxed, they usually hold their tails low and slightly away from their bodies. Lifting the tail high expresses dominance or a tail held straight up and trembling conveys threat to another wolf. A wolf expressing submission holds its tail close to its body and may tuck it between

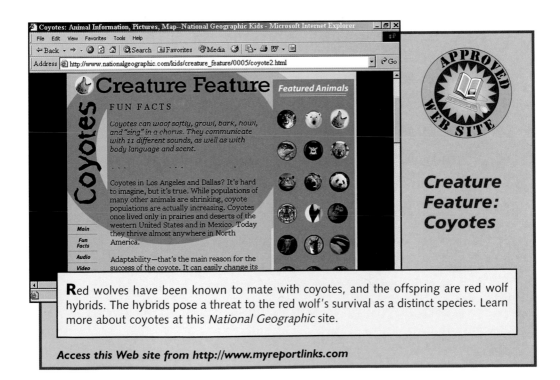

Red wolves have been known to mate with coyotes, and the offspring are red wolf hybrids. The hybrids pose a threat to the red wolf's survival as a distinct species. Learn more about coyotes at this *National Geographic* site.

Access this Web site from http://www.myreportlinks.com

its legs. Wagging a relaxed tail communicates friendliness.

▶ The Howl

The day a wolf pup first howls is an important day in its life. Certainly the howling of wolves has caught the imagination of people since prehistoric times. Scientists have begun to study howls by using scientific equipment so that they can distinguish the notes, pitch, and timing. They have found that each wolf has its own howl; in fact, it has several howls. One scientist listened to the howls of the wolf he raised and believed he could hear a difference in howls of satisfaction after eating and howls of loneliness.[13]

One wolf howling by itself will usually howl several times within about half a minute. When a pack howls, one wolf begins and the others join in, lifting their mouths high. Researchers have noticed that the wolves produce chords, each wolf howling a different note or series of notes. Wolves begin with long, low howls and raise the pitch as they howl. Group howls usually last about a minute and a half.[14]

Wolves seem to howl for a variety of reasons. Some howls seem to signify cries of loneliness. Pack howls, on the other hand, seem to be joyous occasions. Howling may be a way of affirming togetherness and friendship. Observers have seen

A lone red wolf moves through the forest of North Carolina's Alligator River National Wildlife Refuge.

wolves run—tails wagging and eyes bright and excited—to join in a howl. Perhaps the saddest howl is the one that is not answered.

Howls are not the only sound that wolves make. Wolves also bark, although their barks are quieter than a dog's bark. Generally, wolves bark a few times and then stop, rather than barking continuously as dogs do. Wolves growl as they protect their food, and puppies growl as they wrestle among themselves or play with adults.

A friendly wolf sound is a high-pitched squeak. Adult wolves squeak in greeting and to call puppies to come eat or to come for a group nuzzle.

▶ Scent Marking

Wolves seem to communicate with other packs by marking their territory with scents. Trees, rocks, and sticks serve as scent posts. As a wolf pack travels through its territory, wolves urinate on these scent posts, probably to tell other wolves of their presence. One naturalist suggested that wolves could tell from a scent how much time had passed since wolves left the scent. If the scent marker had been left recently, a strange wolf would know to leave quickly. An older scent marker would serve as a sort of yellow light, a "proceed with caution" signal.[15] A wolf passing a scent marker often urinates on top of the previous marker.

Scent posts might also help pack members find each other. Wolves often leave the pack to hunt by themselves and then rejoin the pack later. Checking scent posts might help a single wolf to find the rest of the family.

Hunting

By the time wolf puppies are two or three months old, they have probably left the den to travel with the pack. During the next few months, the puppies stay at a rendezvous site, perhaps with an older family member, while the adults go off to hunt. Wolves usually hunt at dawn and dusk and rest in the middle of the day. The pups waiting at the rendezvous site practice hunting as they pounce on mice or insects—or each other.

By autumn, the pups look like adult wolves and hunt with the pack or by themselves. The red wolves in North Carolina hunt white-tailed deer, raccoons, rabbits, nutria, and mice. When hunting is good, they might eat two to five pounds (one to two kilograms) of food a day.[16]

Dispersal

At the age of six months, young wolves look like adult wolves, although they are still growing and developing. The young wolves usually stay with their family for another year or so. Eventually they leave the family to find their own territory and start a family.

Finding a territory can be risky. Wolf territories are large—a good territory with plentiful prey might be 10,000 to 12,000 acres, or 16 to 19 square miles.[17] Wolves defend their territories from other wolves and might kill strange wolves

▲ These pups will most likely leave their den to travel with their home pack when they are two or three months old until they disperse after they are a year old.

that invade their hunting area. A wolf looking for its own territory has to avoid other wolf packs and find an area that does not belong to another pack.

Dispersing wolves also need to find mates to start their own families. At the age of two or three years, young wolves are ready to breed. The young wolves might look for other single young wolves, or they might join another pack. A zoo-born red wolf released in North Carolina as a pup managed to become the alpha male in an established pack.

Sometimes, biologists serve as matchmakers for the North Carolina red wolves. When some biologists noticed that a three-year-old female had

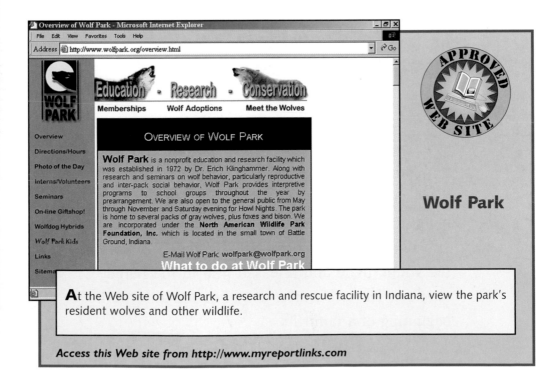

At the Web site of Wolf Park, a research and rescue facility in Indiana, view the park's resident wolves and other wildlife.

Access this Web site from http://www.myreportlinks.com

▲ A red wolf passes in front of its den. Some wolves use the same dens for generations.

established a territory in a fairly remote area, they thought she might have trouble finding a mate there. At the same time, they saw a two-year-old male looking for territory in an area already crowded with wolf packs. The biologists captured the young male and released him in the female's territory. The two wolves soon bonded to form the beginning of a family.[18]

THREATS

Through many centuries, red wolves and American Indians probably lived in the same areas without problems. Wolves are naturally shy, and the American Indians did not keep livestock that the wolves would have hunted.

When Europeans began to arrive in North America, the situation changed quickly. The European settlers knew about wolves, or thought they did, and feared them. Wolves had almost disappeared from the countries these settlers left, but hatred of wolves had been passed down from one generation to the next.

▶ Bounties

As early as 1632, the colony of Virginia passed special legislation rewarding those who killed wolves by giving them the right to kill a wild hog also. In 1668, the colony passed legislation requiring American Indians to kill a certain number of wolves and present the wolves' heads to colonial authorities. The number of wolves to be killed by

Some American Indians not only shared their land with wolves but also revered the species by taking its name. Pictured is Young Hairy Wolf, a member of the Apsaroke, or Crow, Indians, a Rocky Mountain tribe that likened itself to a wolf pack.

each tribe was determined by the number of hunters in the tribe.[1]

As people moved west, and territories became states, state governments paid wolf bounties. In 1858, Iowa passed a law that included a three-dollar bounty for a dead wolf.[2] Individual ranchers and associations of ranchers also paid for dead wolves. Methods of killing wolves ranged from guns to traps and poison. When dens were discovered, pups were pulled out and clubbed to death. Farmers dug pits, suspended boards over them, and baited the traps with meat.

The cruelty sometimes used to destroy wolves seems to be a measure of the hatred people felt toward wolves. For example, two cowboys might suspend a wolf between them and ride in opposite directions to pull it apart. Wolves were burned alive or set free with their jaws wired shut so they would starve.[3] In 1905, a Montana law required wolves to be caught alive and then, under the direction of a veterinarian working for the state, infected with mange, an infectious skin disease caused by mites. These wolves were released so they would pass the contagious disease on to other wolves in their pack.[4]

The Federal Government Steps In

Eventually, ranchers decided to ask the federal government to step in and help kill wolves.

Ranchers reasoned that the wolves were raising their pups on nature reserves—lands that were federally owned—so the federal government should become involved. To the ranchers' way of thinking, it was the government's responsibility to

rid the land of wolves, not theirs alone. The United States Biological Survey (USBS, which later became part of the United States Fish and Wildlife Service) required forest rangers to report the number of wolves they killed in national

In this photograph from 1887, cowboys in Wyoming round up and rope a gray wolf. Wolves were killed in large numbers, especially in the western United States, until laws were enacted to save wolf species.

forests. The federal government also hired bounty hunters to kill wolves. By 1907, forest rangers in thirty-nine national forests reported 1,723 wolves killed.[5]

Between 1915 and 1970, employees of the USBS and later FWS killed almost seventy thousand gray wolves and red wolves.[6] As late as 1963, trappers reported killing more than two thousand red wolves in Louisiana, Texas, Arkansas, and Oklahoma.[7] However, almost all of the animals included in that number were not red wolves but coyotes or wolf-coyote hybrids. By 1963, very few red wolves survived anywhere.

▶ Loss of Habitat

It was not the wolf extermination programs that drove red wolves to the edge of extinction, though. As fields and pastures replaced forests and swamps, the wolves had no place to go. Red wolves seem to be able to adapt to various habitat types, but they still need room to hunt and raise families. A pack's territory can range in size from 10 square miles to 100 square miles (26 square kilometers to 260 square kilometers).[8] When young wolves disperse from the pack, they need to find land that does not "belong" to other wolves. As forests were cleared and roads were built in the eastern states, red wolves retreated westward, but people followed.

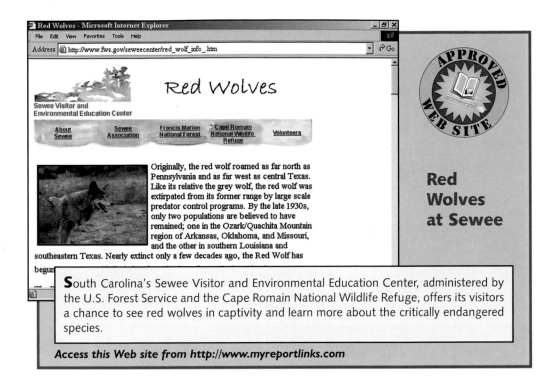

Red Wolves - Microsoft Internet Explorer

File Edit View Favorites Tools Help

Address http://www.fws.gov/seweecenter/red_wolf_info_.htm   Go

Red Wolves

Sewee Visitor and
Environmental Education Center

| About Sewee | Sewee Association | Francis Marion National Forest | Cape Romain National Wildlife Refuge | Volunteers |

Originally, the red wolf roamed as far north as Pennsylvania and as far west as central Texas. Like its relative the grey wolf, the red wolf was extirpated from its former range by large scale predator control programs. By the late 1930s, only two populations are believed to have remained; one in the Ozark/Quachita Mountain region of Arkansas, Oklahoma, and Missouri, and the other in southern Louisiana and southeastern Texas. Nearly extinct only a few decades ago, the Red Wolf has begun

Red Wolves at Sewee

South Carolina's Sewee Visitor and Environmental Education Center, administered by the U.S. Forest Service and the Cape Romain National Wildlife Refuge, offers its visitors a chance to see red wolves in captivity and learn more about the critically endangered species.

Access this Web site from http://www.myreportlinks.com

Woodlands and marshes—and the many animals that lived in them—became harder to find. The wolves that once roamed throughout North America began to disappear. By the middle of the twentieth century, wolves had retreated to remote areas—gray wolves going north to the Canadian border, and red wolves going southwest to the eastern part of Texas. As many as four hundred thousand wolves may have lived in North America before European settlers arrived.[9] Three hundred years later, the population of wolves in the lower forty-eight states numbered just in the hundreds.

▶ Natural Population Controls

Even when wolves roamed freely across the continent, there were far fewer wolves than there were prey animals. Too many wolves in an area will not find enough to eat, so wolves have natural controls on population size.

Wolves themselves may "eliminate" extra wolves. As young wolves leave their families to start new families, they look for open territories— land that has not been claimed by other wolves. When wolves try to hunt in territories used by

http://www.fws.gov/alligatorriver/images/Red Wolf Dad picking up pup.jpg - Microsoft Internet Explorer

File   Edit   View   Favorites   Tools   Help

Address http://www.fws.gov/alligatorriver/images/Red%20Wolf%20Dad%20picking%20up%20pup.jpg   Go

Done

The **Red Wolf Recovery Project** is an effort of the U.S. Fish and Wildlife Service in North Carolina to save and expand the critically endangered red wolf population. Learn more about the project at the Red Wolf Recovery Project Web site, and see more photographs like this one, of a father picking up a pup.

EDITOR'S CHOICE

other wolf packs, they may be accepted into the existing pack. More likely, though, the wolves that were there first will drive the intruder away. Sometimes, wolves kill intruders.

When too many wolves live in an area, the wolves give birth to fewer puppies. David Mech concluded that social pressures limit the number of puppies born. Within a single wolf pack, the alpha female is usually the only one that breeds and has puppies. The wolves that follow the alpha pair respond to the social pressure of the pack and do not breed. When wolf packs feel crowded in an area, a smaller pack may become stressed by the presence of a larger pack to the extent that no wolves in the smaller pack breed and have pups.[10]

Causes of Death

Even in good circumstances, a pair of wolves may raise only a few puppies each year. The mortality rate among infant wolves is about 50 percent. When they are first born, wolves are too small to keep themselves warm and can die from the cold. Pups sometimes die from parasites. Predators, such as eagles and bears, also kill pups.

Disease and parasites kill adult wolves, too. Parasites include worms that live in wolves' intestines, kidneys, or hearts, for example. Even when parasites do not kill wolves directly, they may weaken the wolves so that they are not able to

▲ A red wolf at the Alligator River National Wildlife Refuge.

catch the prey they need to survive. External parasites, including fleas, ticks, and mange mites (which cause wolves to lose their fur), can also weaken wolves.

Through necropsies, or animal autopsies, done on red wolves, scientists know about some of the diseases affecting them. One disease that is known to kill wolves is rabies, a virus that affects the brain. Before animals die from rabies, they lose their fear of humans and develop a tendency to wander and bite at things. Some scientists believe that most incidences of wolves attacking people are a result of rabies. Wolves also die from injuries sustained while attacking prey, in fights with other wolves, or as they defend pups from bears.

▶ Problems of a Small Population

As the red wolves' habitat disappeared, their numbers dwindled. In 1962, one respected mammalogist, or scientist who studies mammals, estimated that the total population of red wolves was less than one hundred. These animals barely survived in a marshy area along the coast of Texas and Louisiana.

The size of a "healthy" population, one that can continue to reproduce and adapt to its environment, depends on the species. Generally speaking, though, zoologists believe that a population of five hundred individuals is needed to keep the species healthy.[11] When the population is too small, problems develop that can doom the species to extinction. The recovery population goal for the red wolf is 550, with 220 wolves in the wild and 330 in captive-breeding facilities.

One problem that may arise in a small population is loss of a balance between males and females. If males make up half of the total population and females make up the other half, most individuals can find mates and reproduce. In a large population, the numbers tend toward being even. However, as fewer puppies are born, chances increase that there will be many more of one sex than the other. If only one quarter of the population is female, only about half of the population will be able to find mates, reproduce, and pass on their genes.

▶ In the Genes

Genes are the basic units of heredity in living organisms, causing animals and people to resemble their parents and grandparents. Genes determine the kinds of proteins an animal, for example, produces, and the proteins, in turn, determine what the animal will look like and how it will act. A gene pool is the total number of genes in a species. Each individual in the species will have some of the genes in the gene pool, but not all of them.

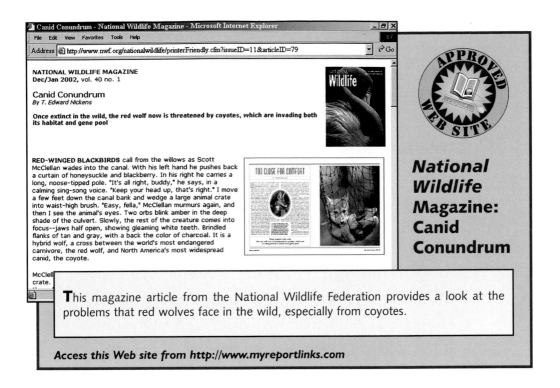

Canid Conundrum - National Wildlife Magazine - Microsoft Internet Explorer

File   Edit   View   Favorites   Tools   Help

Address 🌐 http://www.nwf.org/nationalwildlife/printerFriendly.cfm?issueID=11&articleID=79   ⟳ Go

NATIONAL WILDLIFE MAGAZINE
Dec/Jan 2002, vol. 40 no. 1

Canid Conundrum
By T. Edward Nickens

Once extinct in the wild, the red wolf now is threatened by coyotes, which are invading both its habitat and gene pool

RED-WINGED BLACKBIRDS call from the willows as Scott McClellan wades into the canal. With his left hand he pushes back a curtain of honeysuckle and blackberry. In his right he carries a long, noose-tipped pole. "It's all right, buddy," he says, in a calming sing-song voice. "Keep your head up, that's right." I move a few feet down the canal bank and wedge a large animal crate into waist-high brush. "Easy, fella," McClellan murmurs again, and then I see the animal's eyes. Two orbs blink amber in the deep shade of the culvert. Slowly, the rest of the creature comes into focus--jaws half open, showing gleaming white teeth. Brindled flanks of tan and gray, with a back the color of charcoal. It is a hybrid wolf, a cross between the world's most endangered carnivore, the red wolf, and North America's most widespread canid, the coyote.

McClell
crate.

National Wildlife Magazine: Canid Conundrum

This magazine article from the National Wildlife Federation provides a look at the problems that red wolves face in the wild, especially from coyotes.

Access this Web site from http://www.myreportlinks.com

Over time, a species' gene pool changes. Genes that are harmful tend to disappear, and other genes mutate, or change, to allow the species to adapt to changing circumstances. This process, called genetic drift, works well only if the species' gene pool is made up of a wide variety of genes. As the gene pool becomes smaller, harmful genes last longer, and fewer genes mutate to adapt to change.

In a small population, many of the individuals tend to be related. When related individuals mate and reproduce, they begin a process called inbreeding. Inbreeding means that more of the genes passed from one generation to another are similar. When all the individuals have similar genes, they are all susceptible to the same diseases and less able to adapt to difficult situations. Inbreeding also lowers resistance to disease.

Hybridization

Red wolves found an unusual solution to inbreeding, but it was a solution that would certainly bring an end to the species. As loss of habitat pushed red wolves to the western edge of their territory, they came in contact with coyotes. Coyotes had always lived west of the red wolves, in land that was drier and more open than the forests and wetlands in the eastern

The Nature Conservancy is an environmental organization that strives to protect the plants, animals, and natural communities of earth by preserving habitat. The group has helped preserve lands next to the Alligator River National Wildlife Refuge, home to wild red wolves.

Access this Web site from http://www.myreportlinks.com

states. Historically, wolves kept coyotes out of wolf territories.

With so few red wolves still alive, however, young wolves looking for mates paired with coyotes. Individuals of two different species usually do not mate and produce offspring. If they do, the offspring are sterile—they cannot reproduce. However, wolves and coyotes (and wolves and dogs) are able to mate and produce offspring, which are called hybrids.

The first red wolf–coyote hybrids were probably born in central Texas, along the edge of the two species' territories. However, the absence of wolves has allowed coyotes to migrate eastward. Recently, coyotes were found in the Alligator River National Wildlife Refuge in North Carolina, home of the reintroduced red wolves. In 1996, conservationists realized that some of the pups born in the refuge were hybrids.[12]

Ticking Clock

The IUCN-World Conservation Union maintains a Red List of endangered species around the world. In 2004, the IUCN listed hybridization as the primary threat to the red wolf species. The IUCN report noted that, in order for the North Carolina red wolf population to "maintain 90 percent of its genetic diversity for the next one hundred years," no more than one litter of every fifty-nine litters

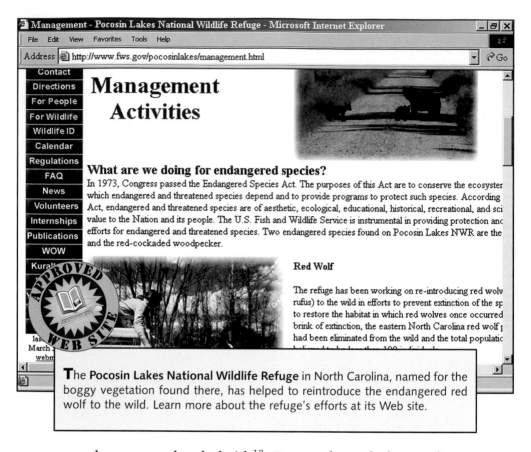

Management - Pocosin Lakes National Wildlife Refuge - Microsoft Internet Explorer

File   Edit   View   Favorites   Tools   Help

Address 🔗 http://www.fws.gov/pocosinlakes/management.html   ▼ 𝒫 Go

Contact
Directions
For People
For Wildlife
Wildlife ID
Calendar
Regulations
FAQ
News
Volunteers
Internships
Publications
WOW
Kura...

Management Activities

What are we doing for endangered species?

In 1973, Congress passed the Endangered Species Act. The purposes of this Act are to conserve the ecosyster which endangered and threatened species depend and to provide programs to protect such species. According Act, endangered and threatened species are of aesthetic, ecological, educational, historical, recreational, and sci value to the Nation and its people. The U.S. Fish and Wildlife Service is instrumental in providing protection and efforts for endangered and threatened species. Two endangered species found on Pocosin Lakes NWR are the and the red-cockaded woodpecker.

Red Wolf

The refuge has been working on re-introducing red wolv rufus) to the wild in efforts to prevent extinction of the sp to restore the habitat in which red wolves once occurred brink of extinction, the eastern North Carolina red wolf ¡ had been eliminated from the wild and the total populatic

The **Pocosin Lakes National Wildlife Refuge** in North Carolina, named for the boggy vegetation found there, has helped to reintroduce the endangered red wolf to the wild. Learn more about the refuge's efforts at its Web site.

born can be hybrid.[13] Researchers believe that there has already been a greater degree of hybridization, however, and they have concluded that hybridization could lead to the disappearance of red wolves as a distinct species in three to six generations, or twelve to fourteen years.[14]

▷ More Threats

Today, all of the wild red wolves live in eastern North Carolina and are at least partially protected by the Endangered Species Act. Despite that protection, humans still threaten their existence.

Not everyone thinks this species should be saved. In 1994, two North Carolina counties passed resolutions demanding that wolves be removed. The counties then took the issue to the courts. In 1995, the North Carolina legislature made it legal to kill wolves on private property. Four wolves were shot over the following months.[15] To address private landowners' concerns, FWS revised federal regulations so that landowners could kill wild red wolves on their property but only when they could provide evidence that a wolf had killed livestock or pets. That same year, a North Carolina senator asked the United States Senate to end payment of federal funds for red wolf recovery. The bill was narrowly defeated.[16]

▶ The Peril of Private Lands

Since the first wolves were released in the Alligator River National Wildlife Refuge, wild wolves have spread out, so that almost 60 percent of the land they use for habitat is privately owned. Since private landowners can do what they want with their land, this habitat could disappear, and lands bordering wildlife refuges could also be developed. When the United States Navy wanted to build a fighter-jet landing field near the Alligator River and Pocosin Lakes refuges, conservation groups took the issue to court and stopped construction of the landing field, at least temporarily.[17]

ROAD TO RECOVERY

Red wolves disappeared from most of their former range during the first half of the twentieth century. Although red wolves had vanished from the Midwestern states where they once hunted, farmers and ranchers still saw "wolves" (at least, they thought the animals were wolves) and killed them when they could. People in Oklahoma, Missouri, and Texas, for example, had no reason to think red wolves were almost extinct. In fact, farmers began to see more wolflike predators.

▶ Mistaken Identity

During the 1950s, one young man began to notice something odd about the red wolves that farmers and ranchers killed. Ranchers had a custom of hanging dead wolves from fences, so it was not difficult for Howard McCarley, a graduate student studying biology, to look carefully at the dead wolves. He noticed that the wolves he saw on ranchers' fences were smaller than the ones he had seen in museums.

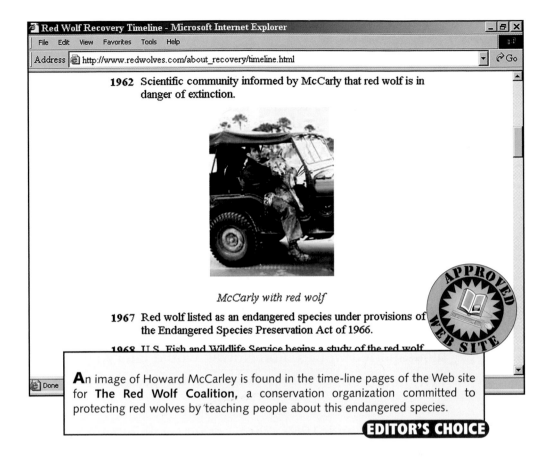

🔲 Red Wolf Recovery Timeline - Microsoft Internet Explorer — 🔲 🔲

File   Edit   View   Favorites   Tools   Help

Address 🔲 http://www.redwolves.com/about_recovery/timeline.html   ▼ 🔲 Go

1962 Scientific community informed by McCarly that red wolf is in danger of extinction.

McCarly with red wolf

1967 Red wolf listed as an endangered species under provisions of the Endangered Species Preservation Act of 1966.

1968 U.S. Fish and Wildlife Service begins a study of the red wolf

An image of Howard McCarley is found in the time-line pages of the Web site for **The Red Wolf Coalition,** a conservation organization committed to protecting red wolves by teaching people about this endangered species.

EDITOR'S CHOICE

McCarley had access to a scientific book published in 1944, *The Wolves of North America,* that provided specific measurements for red wolves, including measurements of their skulls. As McCarley measured the skulls of the wolves killed by ranchers, he noticed that the skulls of the recently killed wolves were smaller than they should be. By 1962, he concluded that these "wolves" were not really wolves at all but wolf-coyote hybrids.[1]

Appeals for Help

Another graduate student, Ronald Nowak, also concluded that the red wolf species was in danger. In 1963, he wrote to the director of the U.S. Fish and Wildlife Service, hoping to bring an end to the government-sponsored hunting of red wolves. The FWS director replied that the red wolf population consisted of four thousand to eight thousand wolves and was not in danger of extinction.[2] Another branch of the government, the Branch of Predator and Rodent Control, still paid trappers to kill red wolves. Nowak's letter arrived the same year that trappers reported killing more than two thousand red wolves. Ron Nowak would later join FWS and become widely respected for his knowledge of wolves.

In 1964 and 1965, three other wolf experts looked for evidence of red wolves in the species' former range. They also found that most of the "wolves" people saw were actually hybrids. But they did find a small population of red wolves along the Gulf Coast of Louisiana and Texas.

As a few scientists began to publish information about the precarious state of the red wolf population, other scientists were writing about other species in danger of extinction, and people began to pay attention. Attitudes were changing. At the beginning of the 1900s, about one third of the people in the United States lived on farms and

▲ A wolf at the Sewee Visitor Center photographed by Lauren Greene, who became interested in nature photography after being given an assignment in a sixth-grade science class. Now the program manager of a nature center in Georgia, she hopes that her photography will inspire others to see the beauty in nature—and the importance of preserving all its species.

ranches. By the 1950s, less than one quarter lived on a farm or ranch.[3] People began to regret the disappearance of woodlands and wildlife—and the hated wolf became a symbol of this loss.

▶ Endangered Species Act

In response to people's concerns about the loss of wildlife and natural landscapes, the FWS compiled a list of species in danger of extinction. In 1966 the United States Congress passed the Endangered Species Protection Act, which was intended to provide some protection for endangered species. Another act, the Endangered Species Conservation Act, followed in 1969. However, neither act was strong enough to be very effective.

In 1973, Congress passed the Endangered Species Act (ESA), which left no doubt that protection of endangered species should be a national priority. The act mandates penalties for killing or harming an individual animal or plant of an endangered species. In addition, it requires federal agencies to make sure that they do not fund or do anything that would harm an endangered species or the species' habitat. With the ESA, Congress made it clear that protection of endangered species might sometimes be more important than "improvements," such as dams, that might benefit people.

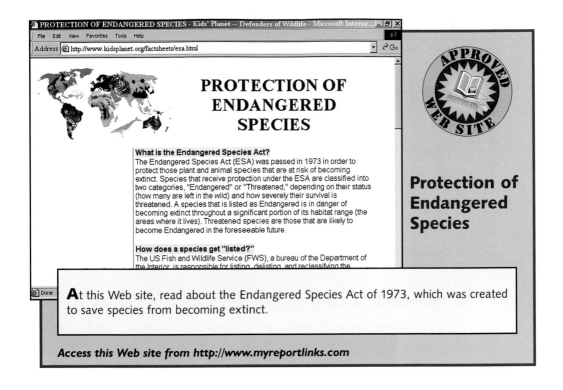

PROTECTION OF ENDANGERED SPECIES - Kids' Planet -- Defenders of Wildlife - Microsoft Interne... ▯�◻▯
File   Edit   View   Favorites   Tools   Help
Address http://www.kidsplanet.org/factsheets/esa.html   ⌐ Go

PROTECTION OF ENDANGERED SPECIES

What is the Endangered Species Act?
The Endangered Species Act (ESA) was passed in 1973 in order to protect those plant and animal species that are at risk of becoming extinct. Species that receive protection under the ESA are classified into two categories, "Endangered" or "Threatened," depending on their status (how many are left in the wild) and how severely their survival is threatened. A species that is listed as Endangered is in danger of becoming extinct throughout a significant portion of its habitat range (the areas where it lives). Threatened species are those that are likely to become Endangered in the foreseeable future.

How does a species get "listed?"
The US Fish and Wildlife Service (FWS), a bureau of the Department of the Interior, is responsible for listing, delisting, and reclassifying the

Protection of Endangered Species

At this Web site, read about the Endangered Species Act of 1973, which was created to save species from becoming extinct.

Access this Web site from http://www.myreportlinks.com

The ESA did more than provide protection for animals and plants. It also required that steps be taken to help endangered species recover, or increase in number. The United States Department of the Interior is responsible for bringing together experts to form a recovery team for each endangered species.

▶ The Red Wolf Recovery Team

Hoping that the Endangered Species Act would become law, FWS established a recovery program for the red wolf just months before the ESA was passed.[4] Curtis Carley became the program's project leader.

At first, the recovery team hoped to help the red wolf species survive in the small area of Louisiana and Texas where it still lived. However, Carley quickly concluded that the wolf-coyote hybrids so greatly outnumbered the pure red wolves that the red wolf species would soon disappear in the wild. The recovery team decided to change course. Instead of protecting red wolves in their habitat, FWS would remove red wolves from their habitat and make them extinct in the wild.

▶ "Planned" Extinction

FWS asked several zoos to submit plans for a red wolf captive-breeding program. The Point Defiance Zoo in Tacoma, Washington, was selected. Several people connected with the Point Defiance Zoo had been concerned about the plight of red wolves for some time. Years earlier, in the 1960s, the zoo received red wolves from other zoos and began a captive-breeding program.[5]

Providing pure red wolves for the new program proved to be difficult, though. One problem was that most of the land that provided habitat for the red wolves was owned by individuals rather than the state or federal government. The recovery program made quick response to any complaints about wild canids a priority. In this way, the recovery team could go onto private land to trap wolves with a landowner's permission.

▶ Will the Real Red Wolves Please Stand?

The team faced another challenge, though. How would they know if a captured wolf was really a wolf and not a hybrid? Red wolves had almost disappeared in the wild before anyone thought to study them. People had differences of opinion about wolf behavior and coyote behavior. But how would hybrids behave? McCarley measured skulls to determine which animals were really wolves, but that method would probably not work for live animals—or would it?

Through a fortunate coincidence, Carley, the program leader, connected with a radiologist who had heard about the use of X-rays in a study of seals. The radiologist suggested the same be done with wolves. Carley identified two hundred red wolf skulls in museums and used measurements from those skulls as a basis for identifying pure red wolves among the animals trapped by the recovery team.[6] In the end, the team decided on eight key indicators, including skull length and width and brain-to-skull ratio, as well as more obvious measurements, such as shoulder height and ear length.[7]

Every trapped animal was measured, weighed, and X-rayed. Animals that did not pass the test were euthanized because the team believed that releasing the coyotes and hybrids would cause problems with the landowners. The skeletons and information about the euthanized animals were sent to the Smithsonian National Museum of Natural History in Washington, D.C., for future reference.[8] Wolves that passed the test were sent to Washington State to be part of the captive-breeding program.

▶ Risks

Both the decision to remove wolves from the wild for captive breeding and the method of deciding which animals were pure wolves carried risks. Because little was known about red wolves, no one could be certain that the wolves would have puppies in captivity. The intent of the Endangered Species Act is to protect species in the wild. Yet there was a chance that FWS would remove all wolves from the wild and then have no puppies to put back into the wild.

Setting standards to determine which animals were pure wolves was also risky. No thorough studies had been done in the past, so no one really knew the range of red wolf sizes. Were some pure red wolves naturally smaller than others? The team took the chance that they might kill all wolves that were a little smaller than the size they considered normal and thus remove their genes from the species' gene pool. Removing certain genes could bring about a change in the species as a whole.

▲ One of the resident red wolves of the Virginia Living Museum, this female gave birth to a pup in the spring of 2006.

During the next few years, the recovery team trapped more than four hundred wild wolflike animals. Only forty-three of those animals were determined to be pure wolves and were sent to the captive-breeding facility in Washington.

▶ A New Life

The wolves' new home was in Graham, Washington, miles from the zoo. A member of the Point Defiance Zoo Society's mammal committee owned a mink farm there, and he made his land available for the wolves.[9] Wolf pairs were released into 10,000-square-foot pens that contained some natural vegetation. Concrete septic tanks provided

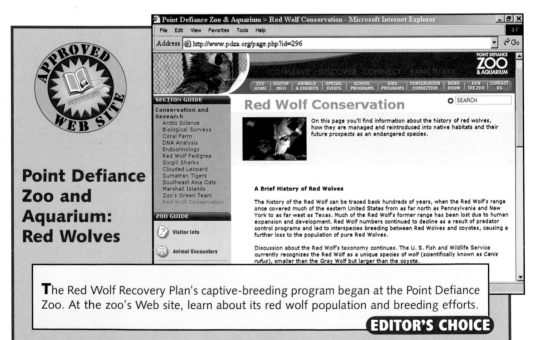

Point Defiance Zoo and Aquarium: Red Wolves

The Red Wolf Recovery Plan's captive-breeding program began at the Point Defiance Zoo. At the zoo's Web site, learn about its red wolf population and breeding efforts.

EDITOR'S CHOICE

Access this Web site from http://www.myreportlinks.com

dens. Instead of hunting wild animals, the wolves learned to eat dry dog-food.

The first question was how well the wolves would do in captivity. Many of them were in a sorry state when they arrived, with internal and external parasites. Some died soon after arrival, but most survived the transfer and grew healthier after receiving veterinary care. None of the first arrivals, however, produced puppies the next spring.

Difficult Beginnings

As the recovery team continued to trap and examine wolflike animals, the captive-breeding program did not look promising. The Point Defiance Zoo's breeding facility already had red wolves when the first wolves captured by the FWS recovery team arrived. Some had been captured in the wild, and others had come from zoos. Six wolves had produced eight puppies. When these red wolves were measured against the new FWS criteria, though, most appeared to be hybrids—including the ones that bred and all of their puppies. Eleven of the seventeen "wolves" at the facility had to be killed.[10]

In 1975 and 1976, none of the captured wolves managed to raise a healthy pup. Finally, in 1977, several pairs of red wolves had puppies. However, many of these puppies lived less than a month.

Hookworms appeared to be one cause, although people caring for the wolves had little opportunity to examine the dead pups—their parents ate them after they died.[11]

The wolves had five litters of pups in 1978, and caretakers gave these puppies medicine, including medication to kill the hookworms, when the pups were ten days old. The pups seemed to be doing well until suddenly, when the pups were about three months old, they began to die. The pups had parvovirus, a contagious disease that also affects dogs. Twelve pups from the five litters survived.[12]

▶ Finding Founders

As the forty-three captured wolves produced puppies, the recovery team realized that not all of them were pure red wolves. Sometimes the pups in one litter would look very different from one another, a clear indication that they were hybrids. Caretakers examined and measured each pup every three months. When the pups were a year old, the recovery team decided whether they should be kept in the program or killed. Parents of hybrid pups also had to be removed from the breeding program, but it was difficult to tell which parent was the hybrid. Sometimes the only way to see which wolf in a mated pair was hybrid was to separate the pair, give them new mates, and then look at the pups. Remains of all the animals

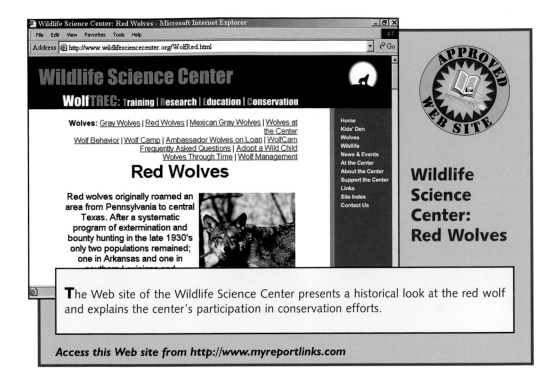

The Web site of the Wildlife Science Center presents a historical look at the red wolf and explains the center's participation in conservation efforts.

Access this Web site from http://www.myreportlinks.com

destroyed and their records are preserved at the University of Puget Sound in Tacoma, Washington.[13]

As the breeding program progressed, the FWS recovery team realized that only seventeen of the forty-three captured wolves were pure wolves. Only fourteen of those wolves bred and produced pups. These fourteen wolves are known as founders. All red wolves alive today are their descendants.

WILD AGAIN

As the U.S. Fish and Wildlife Service Red Wolf Recovery Team trapped red wolves in Texas and Louisiana and shipped them to Washington, team members looked for places to release captive wolves back into the wild. The team decided to try a release on an island, thinking that the wolves would not leave. They chose Bulls Island, a 5,000-acre island in the Cape Romain National Wildlife Refuge along the coast of South Carolina.

▶ Island Experiment

In November 1976, a pair of wild-caught red wolves traveled by plane, truck, and boat from Tacoma, Washington, to a 2,500-square-foot pen on Bulls Island. The wolves were kept in that enclosure for a little less than six weeks and released on December 13.[1]

Bulls Island is surrounded not by deep water but by marsh. At low tide, the wolves could easily walk and swim from Bulls Island to neighboring

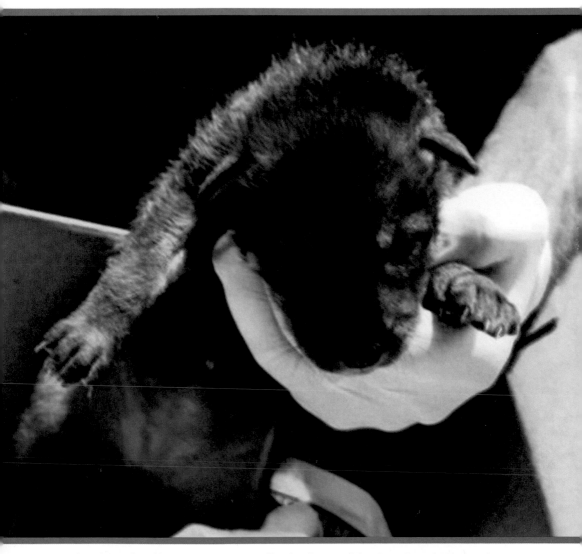

▲ This red wolf pup was born on Bulls Island, part of the Cape Romain National Wildlife Refuge. Bulls Island played an important role in red wolf recovery and was the first island breeding site for the species.

islands. They could also reach the mainland, only three miles (five kilometers) away, and that is just what they did. Just nine days after being released, the female appeared on the mainland. Carley and another team member chased her for forty hours before they caught her.[2] Both wolves were removed from the island.

The recovery team had chosen an island setting to keep the wolves away from people, but the plan had failed. Team members thought they had learned from the experience and decided to try again. In July 1977, they brought another pair of wolves to Bulls Island. This time, the wolves were kept in the pen for six months to give them more time to get used to the area. When they were released, the wolves stayed on Bulls Island and a neighboring island for more than eight months. The team considered this experiment a success, but the release was never meant to be permanent. The wolves were captured and returned to captivity.[3]

▶ Finding a Home

The red wolves needed a large mainland setting where they could spread out and raise families. For red wolves to survive in the wild, the species needed an area large enough for many animals so that all the genes from the founders could be present in the population.

▲ *This red wolf at the Sewee Visitor Center is the mate to the red wolf pictured on page 67. Red wolves in captivity are usually kept together in breeding pairs.*

Recovery team members considered sites in Florida and Georgia. Eventually, they decided on land owned by the Tennessee Valley Authority (TVA), the nation's largest public power company, in western Tennessee and eastern Kentucky. At meetings with state wildlife agencies, FWS team members discussed details of the reintroduction plan. Finally, in 1982, FWS approved a plan. A year later, the board of the TVA also approved the plan. It was only then, in 1983, that the general public learned of the plan from news reports and public meetings held in both Tennessee and Kentucky.

Not on This Land

Public reaction was not positive. Hunters had used the land for years, and they thought the presence of an endangered species would mean they could no longer hunt in the area. Livestock owners thought the wolves would kill their animals, and environmentalists protested because the plan called for killing all the coyotes in the area to prevent wolves and coyotes from interbreeding. As a result of negative public reaction, the state agencies in Tennessee and Kentucky rejected the plan.[4] After years of work, the Red Wolf Recovery Team realized that the wolves could not be released on lands owned by the TVA.

▶ Alligator River National Wildlife Refuge

Just a few months after Tennessee and Kentucky rejected the red wolf reintroduction plan, another possible release site became available. The Prudential Insurance Company owned 118,000 acres of marshland in North Carolina. Plans for use of the land had fallen through, and with the help of the Nature Conservancy, an environmental group, Prudential transferred the land to the Fish and Wildlife Service.[5] The new wildlife refuge, the Alligator River National Wildlife Refuge, offered several advantages for a wolf reintroduction project. It was a peninsula, surrounded by water on

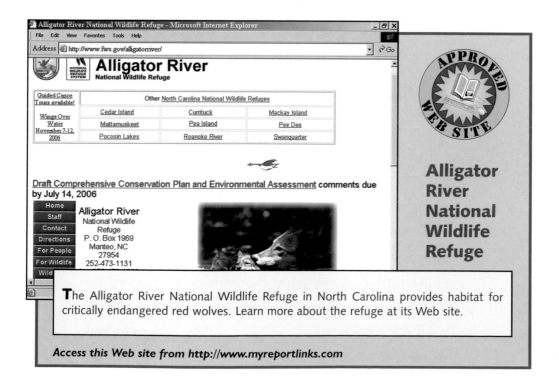

The Alligator River National Wildlife Refuge in North Carolina provides habitat for critically endangered red wolves. Learn more about the refuge at its Web site.

Access this Web site from http://www.myreportlinks.com

three sides, and the few people who lived in the surrounding area did not raise livestock. A navy bombing-practice range in the middle of the refuge kept people away from the area. As FWS experts evaluated the land, they decided that it had enough small animals, such as mice and opossums, to provide food for the wolves. They also found no evidence of coyotes in the area.

▶ Gaining Public Support

The Red Wolf Recovery Team had learned from its experience in Tennessee and Kentucky. In order for a reintroduction plan to work, local people had to support it—or at least not protest it. Team members met with national environmental groups, state wildlife agencies, the governor's staff, local elected officials, and private individuals, including hunters.

A 1982 amendment to the Endangered Species Act made the reintroduction a little easier for local people to accept. The amendment allowed FWS to classify the released wolves as an "experimental, nonessential" population. This classification meant that local people would not face penalties for accidentally killing a wolf. It also allowed people to chase wolves away from their property. According to FWS, the released wolves were "nonessential" because there were about eighty captive red wolves in seven locations.[6]

To make the plan more acceptable to local people, FWS paid the 3M Corporation to invent and produce special tracking collars. The collars held darts filled with tranquilizers. At a command from a radio transmitter, the darts would pierce the wolf's skin and tranquilize the animal. The collars also held tiny computers that were supposed to collect information about the wolves' activity. The information could then be retrieved from another computer. The recovery team was determined to prove that the released wolves could be managed.

Reintroduction Begins

In November 1986, four pairs of red wolves arrived at the Alligator River National Wildlife Refuge. Because of the lessons learned ten years earlier on Bulls Island, the recovery team decided to keep the wolves in large pens for six months. The pens were located in different parts of the refuge so that wolves could develop a sense of their territories. Plywood "doghouses" provided shelter, and three biologists lived near the pens to feed the wolves and keep an eye on them.[7]

At first, the caretakers entered the pens each day to feed the wolves dog food. The wolves would not find dog food in the wild, though, and they had to learn not to expect food from people. To prepare the wolves for release, the caretakers

A U.S. Fish and Wildlife Service employee holds two red wolf pups bred in captivity.

put plywood against one side of the pens so the wolves would not see them as they threw dead animals (mostly animals killed on the roads) over the fence. Instead of being fed once a day, the wolves were given meat only once every fourth day to make the animals accustomed to the conditions they might experience in the wild.[8]

Setbacks

The recovery team planned to release the wolves in the spring, a time when young prey animals would provide food. A spring release would also give the wolves time to adjust to the wild before hunting season began in the fall. The recovery team hoped they would be releasing young pups as well. Biologists gave two of the four females contraceptives so they would not have pups in the spring. The other two females did have pups, but none of the pups survived.

As the release date approached, though, the team learned that the special tranquilizer collars were not ready. FWS had promised that the wolves would be released with these collars, so the team had no choice but to wait for them.

Months passed. Finally in mid-September, team workers put the 3M computer/tranquilizer collars and regular radio collars on two wolves and left the door of their pen open. On October 1, the team opened the doors of the other three pens. All eight wolves were free to make new lives in the refuge. They were not wild wolves, though. They had been fed by people, and they were familiar with the sound of cars. The wolves often walked along the roads in the refuge and refused to move when cars came. One wolf went up to a hunter, who assumed it was someone's dog because it was wearing a collar. When the hunter saw the darts in the collar, he knew he was looking at a wolf and yelled to chase it away.[9]

▶ More Problems Arise

About a month after the first wolves were released, two wolves wandered out of the refuge and had to be recaptured. A male walked to a nearby town, perhaps in search of dog food. When he was finally recaptured, team members saw that he had lost eleven pounds (five kilograms) in his month of freedom. They also learned that the 3M tranquilizer collar did not work.[10]

Gradually, the wolves grew wilder, although more than half of the eight wolves did not survive the first year. A female died from an infection, another female had to be euthanized after being injured by other wolves, and two males were hit by cars. A female that gave birth to a litter of pups in the spring died of complications from the birth. The recovery team expected that her pups would die of starvation, but they later learned that her mate had raised a pup by himself.[11] Another female also gave birth to pups in the spring, and one pup from that litter survived.

The recovery team brought more wolves to the Alligator River National Wildlife Refuge, and more pups were born there. Still, by 1990, only nine adult wolves and a few pups lived in the marshy woodlands.[12]

▶ Great Smoky Mountains National Park

In 1990, FWS began preparations for releasing wolves into the Great Smoky Mountains National Park, straddling North Carolina and Tennessee.

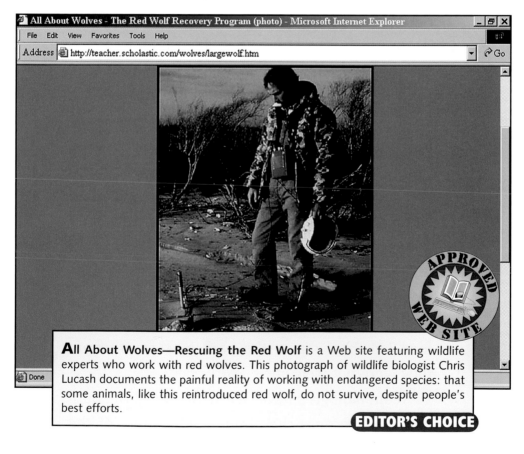

All About Wolves - The Red Wolf Recovery Program (photo) - Microsoft Internet Explorer

File   Edit   View   Favorites   Tools   Help

Address http://teacher.scholastic.com/wolves/largewolf.htm   Go

All About Wolves—Rescuing the Red Wolf is a Web site featuring wildlife experts who work with red wolves. This photograph of wildlife biologist Chris Lucash documents the painful reality of working with endangered species: that some animals, like this reintroduced red wolf, do not survive, despite people's best efforts.

EDITOR'S CHOICE

The recovery team thought the large expanses of steep, forested land would provide space for the wolves to roam freely. They released the first wolves in the park in 1991. By 1996, another thirty-seven wolves had been released.[13]

FWS knew that coyotes lived in the park, but biologists wanted to know if an established red wolf population could live near coyotes without interbreeding.[14] Biologists believe that animals will choose to mate with their own species when they can.

An Unsuitable Site

Before the recovery team could learn about inter-actions between red wolves and coyotes, however, they realized that the release site was not as good for the wolves as they first thought. Twenty-six of the thirty-seven released wolves either died or had to be captured after they wandered onto private land. Worse, no puppies survived in the wild although at least twenty-eight puppies were born in the park and were not removed.[15]

The team's biologists concluded that the wolves could not find enough to eat in the steep mountain terrain inside the park. The search for food led them out of the park into areas where they were not welcome.

Team biologists never learned why all the pup-pies died because they found only a few of the

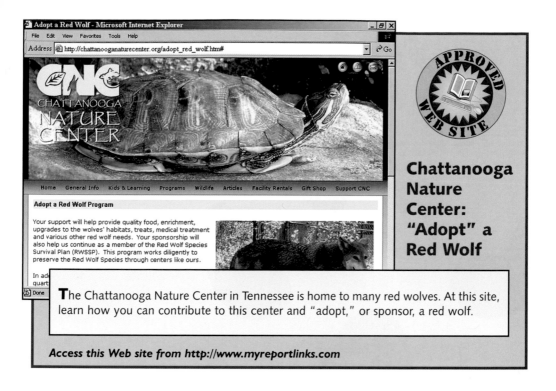

Home   General Info   Kids & Learning   Programs   Wildlife   Articles   Facility Rentals   Gift Shop   Support CNC

Adopt a Red Wolf Program

Your support will help provide quality food, enrichment, upgrades to the wolves' habitats, treats, medical treatment and various other red wolf needs. Your sponsorship will also help us continue as a member of the Red Wolf Species Survival Plan (RWSSP). This program works diligently to preserve the Red Wolf Species through centers like ours.

In ad
quart

Chattanooga Nature Center: "Adopt" a Red Wolf

The Chattanooga Nature Center in Tennessee is home to many red wolves. At this site, learn how you can contribute to this center and "adopt," or sponsor, a red wolf.

Access this Web site from http://www.myreportlinks.com

dead puppies to examine. One pup had died from parvovirus, which had probably killed other pups in its litter. Coyotes killed another pup. Biologists assume that some pups starved because their parents were not able to find enough food.

In 1998, the recovery team decided to end attempts to establish a wild population in the Great Smoky Mountains National Park.

▶ Finally, Success

As the recovery team captured the remaining wolves in the Great Smoky Mountains National Park, the wolves in eastern North Carolina were doing well. By 1992, pups born in the wild had

A red wolf's footprint. Wolves and other wild canids tend to walk in a straight path, while dogs move from side to side.

grown and had their own pups. The following year, wolves were released in Pocosin Lakes National Wildlife Refuge to extend the wild red wolves' range. In 1995, researchers at North Carolina State University conducted an attitude survey and found that a majority of the people who lived near the red wolves supported red wolf introduction.[16]

CAPTIVE BREEDING

The Point Defiance Zoo's captive-breeding program began slowly. As the red wolves grew accustomed to their new surroundings, they mated and gave birth to pups. Biologists learned about care of the wolves and their puppies and were able to help more pups survive.

Soon, the Red Wolf Recovery Team had to find additional space for their wolves, and they contacted zoos around the country to see if they had room to care for the wolves. Usually, zoos that agree to take wolves receive a mated pair. Puppies raised by the pair are then sent to other locations. For example, the Texas Zoo first received a mated pair of wolves in 1989. Seventeen wolf pups have been born there.[1]

▶ The Species Survival Plan

In 1984, the American Zoo and Aquarium Association (AZA) agreed to accept the red wolf into its Species Survival Plan (SSP) program. Begun in 1981, this program allows zoos throughout the country to work together to help a species

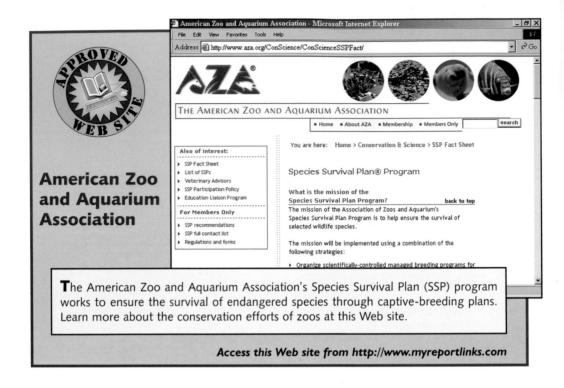

American Zoo and Aquarium Association

The American Zoo and Aquarium Association's Species Survival Plan (SSP) program works to ensure the survival of endangered species through captive-breeding plans. Learn more about the conservation efforts of zoos at this Web site.

Access this Web site from http://www.myreportlinks.com

survive through carefully planned breeding. The Species Survival Plan also helps to educate the public about the species and the challenges it faces. Each SSP has a coordinator and a committee of experts to help direct the plan.[2]

Basic to every SSP is the studbook, which is a computerized database that contains information about each animal born in the program. Scientists can then use the computer to sort and analyze this information and then plan how wolves should be paired for breeding. Facts about puppies, such as their gender and their parents, are added to the studbook soon after the pups are born, and each pup is given a number. As wolves are paired with other wolves or moved to different locations, this information is added to the database.

▶ Preserving the Gene Pool

The database is a valuable tool for scientists as they work with an endangered species. As a species' population gets smaller, so does the species' gene pool. The goal of an SSP is to keep the gene pool as large as possible. Zoologists identify animals with rare genes and carefully match them with mates to keep those genes in the gene pool.

When the recovery team measured and X-rayed animals to determine which were pure red wolves, the biologists took all but seventeen animals out of the breeding program. Of the seventeen wolves, only fourteen mated to produce puppies. All of the red wolves managed by the Fish and Wildlife Service and AZA are descended from these fourteen founder wolves. With so few founders, preserving the diversity of the gene pool is especially important. Computers and modern science, especially recent developments in the study of genes, allow biologists to track the progress of the species from one generation to another.

The studbook provides additional information as well. Scientists can use computer programs to look at trends in the population, such as survival

▲ All of the pure red wolves alive today are descendants of fourteen founder wolves. This female red wolf, photographed at the Virginia Living Museum, is one such descendant.

rates of wolves born from parents of a specific age or the balance of males and females in a group.

A husbandry manual is also an important part of the SSP. This manual provides guidelines for the care of animals based on scientific information. All zoos participating in an SSP follow these guidelines so that all animals in the plan receive the same kind of care and are fed the same kind of food. This consistency makes it easier to detect health problems and to transfer animals from one location to another.

The Program Expands

By 1985, as FWS developed plans to release captive wolves into the Alligator River National Wildlife Refuge, sixty-five red wolves lived in six locations. In 2002, approximately one hundred seventy-five wolves lived in captivity at thirty-three facilities.[3] By 2006, thirty-eight zoos and breeding facilities provided homes for captive red wolves. The Point Defiance Zoo breeding facility is still the largest breeding facility, with thirty-five wolves in January 2006.[4] The Wild Canid Survival

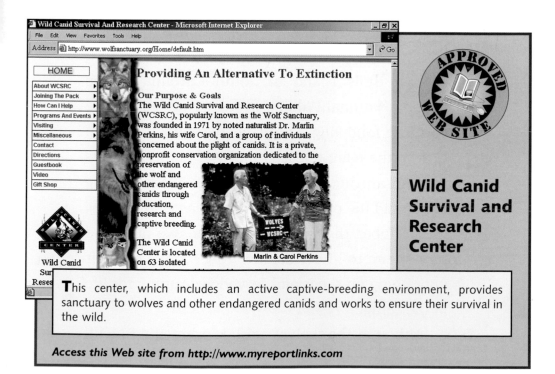

This center, which includes an active captive-breeding environment, provides sanctuary to wolves and other endangered canids and works to ensure their survival in the wild.

Access this Web site from http://www.myreportlinks.com

and Research Center in Eureka, Missouri, provides space for several mated pairs. Most zoos have room for only one pair of captive wolves.

Once a year, representatives from these facilities get together to discuss the progress of captive breeding and how best to proceed. Representatives might decide that one red wolf should be moved to another location to be mated with a particular wolf. Or they might decide that a particular wolf should not breed at all the next year because that wolf's genes are overrepresented in the gene pool and the program has limited space.

▶ Learning to Be Wild

In November 1987, the recovery team added another dimension to the captive-breeding program. The team took a mated pair of wolves to a pen on Bulls Island in South Carolina's Cape Romain National Wildlife Refuge. Four pups were born the following April, and two pups survived. In July, the team released the wolf family from its pen. An alligator killed the mother wolf, but the father and the pups learned to live as wild wolves. In December, the team captured the two pups and sent them to the Alligator River refuge. Their upbringing on the island served as training for life in the refuge.[5]

Although the wolves raised in breeding facilities are usually healthy and strong and protected from alligators, they are not wild. They do not need to find their own food, and they may not be afraid of people. Kim Scott, the assistant director of the Wild Canid Survival and Research Center, explained that when the zoologists choose wolves to release in the wild, they look for "natural behaviors," such as digging their own dens. The center provides boxes, but wolves often dig underground dens. They do not choose wolves that seem too comfortable in captivity.[6]

Still, being taught by their parents to hunt prey is the best training for young wolves. In 1989, the

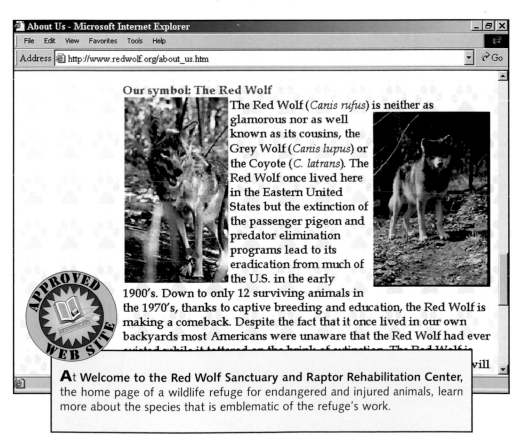

About Us - Microsoft Internet Explorer

File   Edit   View   Favorites   Tools   Help

Address http://www.redwolf.org/about_us.htm   Go

Our symbol: The Red Wolf

The Red Wolf (*Canis rufus*) is neither as glamorous nor as well known as its cousins, the Grey Wolf (*Canis lupus*) or the Coyote (*C. latrans*). The Red Wolf once lived here in the Eastern United States but the extinction of the passenger pigeon and predator elimination programs lead to its eradication from much of the U.S. in the early 1900's. Down to only 12 surviving animals in the 1970's, thanks to captive breeding and education, the Red Wolf is making a comeback. Despite the fact that it once lived in our own backyards most Americans were unaware that the Red Wolf had ever

At Welcome to the Red Wolf Sanctuary and Raptor Rehabilitation Center, the home page of a wildlife refuge for endangered and injured animals, learn more about the species that is emblematic of the refuge's work.

recovery team sent another female to join the male on Bulls Island. The next spring, the wolves had five pups. An alligator killed this mother and one pup, but the father again raised the remaining pups. Then a hurricane severely damaged the little island in September. Although the father and his four pups survived the hurricane, the father was probably injured because he died soon after the hurricane hit.[7]

Other Releases

Island breeding has disadvantages as well as advantages. The total population of red wolves is still small enough that biologists do not want to lose any wolves, and wolves die in the wild. However, the recovery team continued to take advantage of the opportunity to raise wild wolves. During the sixteen years that Bulls Island provided a home for red wolf pairs, twenty-six pups were born there.[8]

In 1990, the recovery team released a pair of wolves in St. Vincent National Wildlife Refuge, a barrier island off the coast of Florida in the Gulf of Mexico. For several years, mated wolf pairs were released on Horn Island, part of the Gulf Islands National Seashore, eight miles (thirteen kilometers) from mainland Mississippi. In 1998, FWS decided not to keep wolves on Horn Island because it was more likely that wolves would meet human visitors there.[9]

▶ A New Emphasis on Captive Breeding

When the FWS recovery team began to remove red wolves from the marshy coastline of Texas and Louisiana, the goal was simply to protect the species in captivity until the wolves could be released into the wild again. By 1999, experts realized that the original goal did not fit the real-world circumstances.

FWS asked the Conservation Breeding Specialist Group of the IUCN-World Conservation Union to help with a meeting that would bring

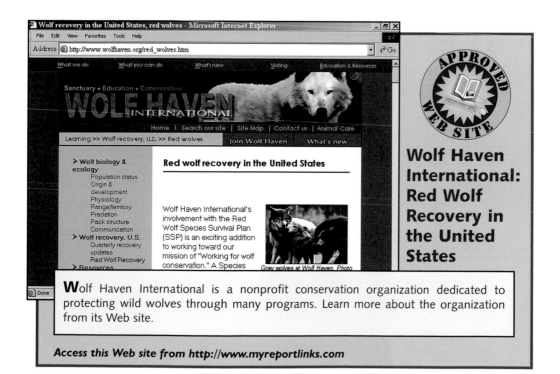

Wolf recovery in the United States, red wolves - Microsoft Internet Explorer

File Edit View Favorites Tools Help

Address http://www.wolfhaven.org/red_wolves.htm   Go

What we do   What you can do   What's new   Visiting   Education & Resources

Sanctuary • Education • Conservation

WOLF HAVEN INTERNATIONAL

Home | Search our site | Site Map | Contact us | Animal Care

Learning >> Wolf recovery, U.S. >> Red wolves   Join Wolf Haven   What's new

➤ Wolf biology & ecology
   Population status
   Origin & development
   Physiology
   Range/territory
   Predation
   Pack structure
   Communication
➤ Wolf recovery, U.S.
   Quarterly recovery updates
   Red Wolf Recovery
➤ Resources

Red wolf recovery in the United States

Wolf Haven International's involvement with the Red Wolf Species Survival Plan (SSP) is an exciting addition to working toward our mission of "Working for wolf conservation." A Species

Gray wolves at Wolf Haven. Photo

Done

Wolf Haven International: Red Wolf Recovery in the United States

APPROVED WEB SITE

Wolf Haven International is a nonprofit conservation organization dedicated to protecting wild wolves through many programs. Learn more about the organization from its Web site.

Access this Web site from http://www.myreportlinks.com

scientific experts together to plan the future course of the red wolf recovery program. IUCN began in 1948 as the International Union for the Protection of Nature. The international organization later changed its name to the World Conservation Union as it continued to provide information about species in danger of extinction and about the environment and ways to protect it.

In April 1999, the Conservation Breeding Specialist Group (SSC/IUCN) and the U.S. Fish and Wildlife Service conducted a workshop titled "Population and Habitat Viability Assessment for the Red Wolf."[10] Participants decided on five key issues that needed to be resolved as they planned the future of the recovery program. The issues included monitoring the wild red wolves in North Carolina and finding new locations for captive breeding.

▶ The Hybrid Threat

The experts soon realized that one issue—the threat of losing the species because of crossbreeding with coyotes—affected every other issue.[11] Workshop participants came to the conclusion that captive breeding was more important than ever for several reasons. Captive breeding is the only way to ensure that pups are authentic red wolves and not hybrids as long as red wolves cannot be kept separate from coyotes in the wild. Captive breeding is also necessary to increase the wild population in the hope that a large population of red wolves will keep coyotes out of their territory. In addition, captive breeding is required for research. Scientists need to continue to study the red wolf genome, or the complete genetic makeup of each individual, as well as the methods of ensuring diversity in the gene pool, but they also need to study the hybrids.

Some biologists wonder if hybridization is a natural process that will change the red wolf species and make it more adaptable. Perhaps the two species should be allowed to mate and have pups. The workshop participants decided that

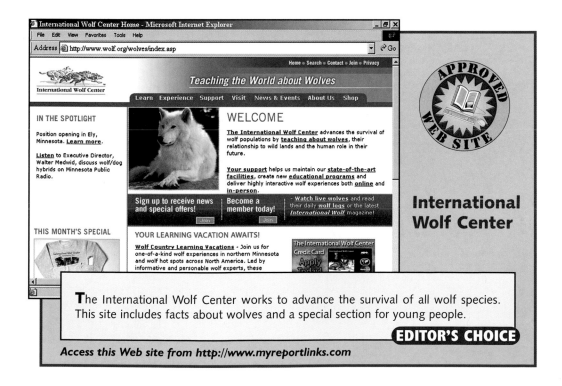

The International Wolf Center works to advance the survival of all wolf species. This site includes facts about wolves and a special section for young people.

EDITOR'S CHOICE

Access this Web site from http://www.myreportlinks.com

they need to know more about hybrids. In the short term, biologists will continue to identify hybrids in the wild population by taking blood samples from the animals and sending them to a lab where DNA tests reveal their genetic makeup. In the long term, they need to know if the hybrid population is viable. In other words, can the hybrids reproduce over a span of generations and continue to have healthy pups?[12]

The scientists concluded that hybrids should be studied when space is available. However, their first goal was finding more space to breed red wolves. In addition, they emphasized the importance of using new techniques to freeze semen from male wolves for use in the future and ways to introduce genes of wolves that have died into the gene pool.

Science continues to open doors for the zoologists striving to maintain a healthy gene pool of red wolves. However, difficulties finding space for captive wolves continues to limit the program.

Red wolves might have slipped quietly into extinction if a few individuals had not been paying attention during the 1960s and 1970s. Most people back then had never heard of a red wolf—and most of those who knew anything about red wolves considered them pests or a danger, something to be destroyed.

But the concerns of those who cared about the endangered red wolf reached the U.S. Fish and Wildlife Service. Armed with the new Endangered Species Act, FWS in the form of Curtis Carley descended on the Texas marshes where the last red wolves lived and lifted them to safety in Washington State. It was a daring rescue. Making a species extinct in the wild in order to save it for the future had never been done before. No one could be certain the plan would succeed.

Today, the number of living red wolves is still short of the Red Wolf Recovery/Species Survival

Plan's goal of 550 wolves—220 red wolves in the wild and 330 in captivity in at least thirty facilities.[1] Even so, the recovery plan has been dramatically successful.

The Wild Wolves of North Carolina

By 2005, at least one hundred wild red wolves roamed through an area of 1.7 million acres in northeastern North Carolina. Three protected areas, the Alligator River National Wildlife Refuge, Pocosin Lakes National Wildlife Refuge, and Mattamuskeet National Wildlife Refuge, make up 40 percent of the wolves' homeland. The other 60 percent is private property.[2]

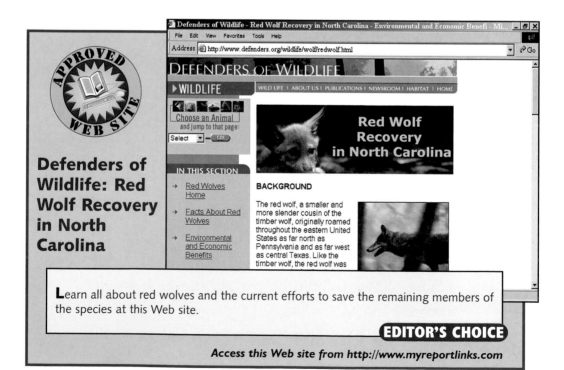

Defenders of Wildlife: Red Wolf Recovery in North Carolina

Learn all about red wolves and the current efforts to save the remaining members of the species at this Web site.

EDITOR'S CHOICE

Access this Web site from http://www.myreportlinks.com

Today, all the wolves born in the recovery zone are wild. Members of the Red Wolf Recovery Program field team hunt for puppies each spring. They tag the pups, take blood samples, and replace the pups in the den. In the fall, they capture all the pups they can find, check their health, vaccinate them, and fit them with radio collars before releasing them again.[3]

While the field team does what it can to keep the wolves healthy, biologists think of ways to keep the species healthy. They use blood samples to monitor the gene pool of the wild population and add wolves to keep the gene pool healthy.

▶ A Bold Experiment

In 2002, the field team placed two captive-born pups into a den with wild-born pups of the same age. Wolf parents had raised foster pups in captivity, and the field team wanted to know if wild wolves would do the same. The two captive pups, a male and a female, came from a litter of six pups born in the North Carolina Zoological Park. Before placing the pups in the wild, zoologists put microchips under their skin so that the field team could identify the pups as they grew.[4]

The red wolf foster mother had two of her own pups in the den. The year before, she raised six pups, so the field team felt confident that she

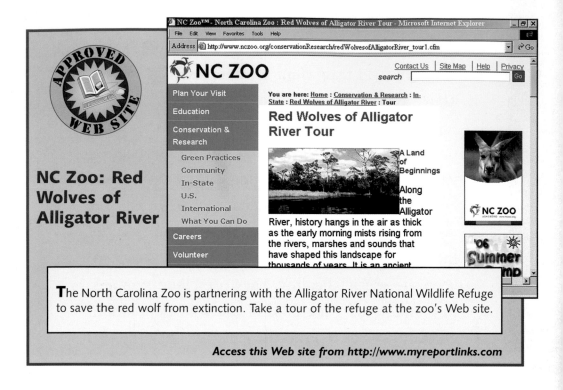

NC Zoo™ - North Carolina Zoo : Red Wolves of Alligator River Tour - Microsoft Internet Explorer

File   Edit   View   Favorites   Tools   Help

Address 🖉 http://www.nczoo.org/conservationResearch/redWolvesofAlligatorRiver_tour1.cfm   ▾ ⌀ Go

Contact Us | Site Map | Help | Privacy

NC ZOO

search [   ] Go

NC Zoo: Red Wolves of Alligator River

Plan Your Visit

Education

Conservation & Research

   Green Practices

   Community

   In-State

   U.S.

   International

   What You Can Do

Careers

Volunteer

You are here: Home : Conservation & Research : In-State : Red Wolves of Alligator River : Tour

Red Wolves of Alligator River Tour

A Land of Beginnings

Along the Alligator River, history hangs in the air as thick as the early morning mists rising from the rivers, marshes and sounds that have shaped this landscape for thousands of years. It is an ancient

🐾 NC ZOO
ASHEBORO www.nczoo.org

'06 ☼
Summer
Camp

The North Carolina Zoo is partnering with the Alligator River National Wildlife Refuge to save the red wolf from extinction. Take a tour of the refuge at the zoo's Web site.

Access this Web site from http://www.myreportlinks.com

could manage four. The foster mother accepted the zoo-born pups as her own.

The two pups thrived. Before he was two years old, the male zoo-born pup joined another pack as the alpha wolf. In the spring of 2004, the field team discovered that he had fathered a litter of eight pups. The female zoo-born pup lived for two years but died in 2004 due to complications with pregnancy.

▶ Adaptive Management Plan

Biologists continue to transfer pups to North Carolina that were raised on islands. By increasing

If the red wolf is to make a substantial recovery, people's fears and misconceptions about wolves in general will need to be addressed.

the number of wild wolves, they hope to keep coyotes away from the wolves.

In 1999, FWS worked with scientists and zoologists to develop an Adaptive Management Plan for the North Carolina wolves. With this plan, biologists hope to learn more about the interbreeding of wolves and coyotes while preserving the red wolf species. They divided the wolves' total area into zones. No coyotes are allowed in Zone 1. When field team members find coyotes in Zone 2, they remove the coyotes or sterilize them and put radio collars on them. These coyotes then hold a territory for future red wolves but will not be able to produce hybrid pups. As the red wolf population expands, the team moves the coyotes to open new territory for the wolves. Scientists monitor the wolves, coyotes, and hybrids in Zone 3 to learn what they can about the crossbreeding of wolves and coyotes.

▶ Public Acceptance

Not all of the red wolves' human neighbors are happy to have them in North Carolina, although studies have shown that most people think the reintroduction is a good idea. In fact, a recent study indicated that the wolves may add to the economy by bringing tourists to see the wild areas and the wild animals that live there.[5]

▲ *Thanks to the efforts of wildlife officials and concerned individuals, red wolves like this one have a chance to run free in the wild—at least, for now. It is up to all of us to make sure that this species and other endangered species do not vanish from the earth forever.*

▶ Challenges

The Red Wolf Recovery Program still faces challenges. More than half of the land used by the red wolves is private property. There is no guarantee the land will be available to the wolves in the future. Increased tourism may help to make wolves more valuable in neighboring communities, but more tourists and more roads will probably increase the number of wolves killed by vehicles.

FWS had hoped to begin three populations of wild wolves. As of 2006, no new location has been identified. The entire population lives in one location, making it more susceptible to a contagious disease or natural catastrophe, such as a hurricane. Because there is little hope of finding a location that will remain free of coyotes, the recovery team is learning what it can in North Carolina about how to prevent red wolf-coyote breeding.

In the meantime, zoos and captive-breeding programs might be all that stand between a strong population of pure red wolves and extinction of the species due to hybridization.

In 1973, Congress took the farsighted step of creating the Endangered Species Act, widely regarded as the world's strongest and most effective wildlife conservation law. It set an ambitious goal: to reverse the alarming trend of human-caused extinction that threatened the ecosystems we all share.

Each book in this series explores the life of an endangered animal. The books tell how and why the animals have become endangered and explain the efforts being made to restore their populations.

The United States Fish and Wildlife Service and the National Marine Fisheries Service share responsibility for administration of the Endangered Species Act. Over time, animals are added to, reclassified in, or removed from the federal list of Endangered and Threatened Wildlife and Plants. At the time of publication, all the animals in this series were listed as endangered species. The most up-to-date list can be found at **http://www.fws.gov/endangered/wildlife.html**.

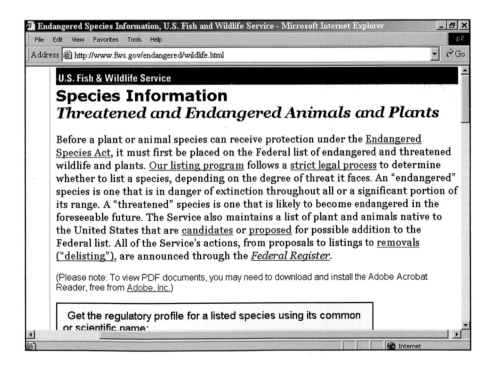

Endangered Species Information, U.S. Fish and Wildlife Service - Microsoft Internet Explorer

File   Edit   View   Favorites   Tools   Help

Address http://www.fws.gov/endangered/wildlife.html

U.S. Fish & Wildlife Service

Species Information
Threatened and Endangered Animals and Plants

Before a plant or animal species can receive protection under the Endangered Species Act, it must first be placed on the Federal list of endangered and threatened wildlife and plants. Our listing program follows a strict legal process to determine whether to list a species, depending on the degree of threat it faces. An "endangered" species is one that is in danger of extinction throughout all or a significant portion of its range. A "threatened" species is one that is likely to become endangered in the foreseeable future. The Service also maintains a list of plant and animals native to the United States that are candidates or proposed for possible addition to the Federal list. All of the Service's actions, from proposals to listings to removals ("delisting"), are announced through the *Federal Register*.

(Please note: To view PDF documents, you may need to download and install the Adobe Acrobat Reader, free from Adobe, Inc.)

Get the regulatory profile for a listed species using its common or scientific name:

Internet

Report Links

The Internet sites described below can be accessed at
http://www.myreportlinks.com

▶**Defenders of Wildlife: Red Wolf Recovery in North Carolina**
Editor's Choice Visit this Web site for comprehensive information about red wolves.

▶**Red Wolf Recovery Project**
Editor's Choice Learn about the U.S. Fish and Wildlife Service's efforts to save the red wolf.

▶**The Red Wolf Coalition**
Editor's Choice Browse the site of a volunteer organization dedicated to saving red wolves.

▶**International Wolf Center**
Editor's Choice Explore the Web site of an international organization dedicated to wolves.

▶**All About Wolves—Rescuing the Red Wolf**
Editor's Choice This site offers information from experts involved in red wolf recovery efforts.

▶**Point Defiance Zoo and Aquarium: Red Wolves**
Editor's Choice Learn about red wolves at the Point Defiance Zoo in Washington.

▶**Alligator River National Wildlife Refuge**
View the Web site of the Alligator River National Wildlife Refuge.

▶**American Zoo and Aquarium Association**
Learn how the American Zoo and Aquarium Association (AZA) helps species survive.

▶**Animal Facts: Red Wolf**
A North Carolina nature center is home to red wolves.

▶**ARKive: Red wolf (Canis rufus)**
View photographs and videos of red wolves on this Web site.

▶**Chattanooga Nature Center: "Adopt" a Red Wolf**
Learn how you can "adopt," or sponsor, a red wolf.

▶**Creature Feature: Coyotes**
Learn more about coyotes at this National Geographic site.

▶**"The Far Reach of David Mech"**
Read about one of the foremost wildlife biologists studying wolves today.

▶**Field Trip Earth: Red Wolves of Alligator River**
Learn about the wild red wolves of the Alligator River refuge.

▶**National Wildlife Magazine: Canid Conundrum**
Read this article to learn about efforts to save the red wolf.

Report Links

The Internet sites described below can be accessed at
http://www.myreportlinks.com

▶**The Nature Conservancy**
Learn more about the Nature Conservancy from its Web site.

▶**NC Zoo: Red Wolves of Alligator River**
Explore North Carolina's Alligator River refuge, where red wolves are being saved.

▶**Pocosin Lakes National Wildlife Refuge**
Another North Carolina refuge is working to save the red wolf.

▶**Protection of Endangered Species**
Read more about the Endangered Species Act.

▶**Red Wolves at Sewee**
A South Carolina center works to restore the red wolf population.

▶**The Sacramento Zoo: Animals as Symbols**
Wolves, among other animals, suffer from a bad reputation because of myths and legends.

▶**USFWS Endangered Species Program Kid's Corner**
This USFWS Web site offers ways you can help save endangered species.

▶**Virginia Living Museum**
Visit a Virginia museum where the animals look back at you.

▶**Welcome to the Red Wolf Sanctuary and Raptor Rehabilitation Center**
Visit the Web site of the Red Wolf Sanctuary and Raptor Rehabilitation Center.

▶**Wild Canid Survival and Research Center**
Explore the Web site of the Wild Canid Survival and Research Center.

▶**Wildlife Science Center: Red Wolves**
Learn about the red wolf and efforts to save the species.

▶**Wolf Haven International: Red Wolf Recovery in the United States**
This nonprofit organization works for wolf survival.

▶**Wolf History: Wolves in the Fossil Record**
Learn about the evolution of canids by exploring the fossil record.

▶**Wolf Park**
A nonprofit research facility in Indiana houses wolves.

▶**Write Your Representative**
Find links to your congressional representatives on this government site.

alpha wolf—The leader of a wolf pack. Wolf packs usually have an alpha male and an alpha female. Often, but not always, the alpha wolves are parents of the other wolves in the pack.

carnassials—The specialized teeth of carnivores (meat-eating animals) that cut through flesh to bite off chunks of meat.

disperse—Young red wolves usually leave their parents, or disperse, sometime between the ages of one and two years. When young wolves disperse, they search for a mate and their own territory.

DNA (deoxyribonucleic acid)—A molecule that carries the genes that make the young of a species like their parents.

dominance—The social position of certain wolves in relation to other wolves within a wolf pack. Wolf packs are organized according to a social hierarchy in which each wolf has a certain rank. A wolf that has a higher social rank than another wolf is dominant over that wolf. The other wolf is submissive.

euthanize—To put to death painlessly.

founders—The members of a species from which all others are descended. All the red wolves alive today are descended from fourteen founders.

gene—The basic unit of heredity. All of the genes in one individual are the individual's genome.

gene pool—The total number of genes, including alternative forms of genes called alleles, in a species.

hierarchy—A system that ranks one above another. Wolf packs have a social hierarchy with the alpha wolf at the top. Another wolf might be submissive to the alpha wolf but dominant over another wolf.

hybrid—The offspring of different species. When a red wolf and a coyote mate, the pups are hybrids.

hybridization—The breeding across species that produces hybrids.

litter—All of the young born together. Red wolves usually give birth to litters of two to six pups. The pups in a litter are littermates.

nutria—Large rodents with webbed hind feet that live part of the time in water.

prey—Animals hunted for food. The red wolves in North Carolina hunt white-tailed deer, raccoons, rabbits, mice, and other animals.

recovery plan—A plan to help an endangered species recover, or become more numerous. The Endangered Species Act of 1973 requires that the Department of the Interior brings together scientists and other people who are knowledgeable about an endangered species to develop a plan to help that species recover.

regurgitate—Vomit. Adult wolves bring up partially digested food from their stomachs to feed young pups.

Species Survival Plan—A plan developed by the American Zoo and Aquarium Association to help zoos protect an endangered species. The plan helps zoos and other facilities plan the breeding of captive animals to preserve as much as possible of the species' gene pool.

Chapter 1. The Last Wolves

1. L. David Mech, *The Wolf: The Ecology and Behavior of an Endangered Species* (Minneapolis: University of Minnesota Press, 1970), p. 20.

2. Peter Steinhart, *The Company of Wolves* (New York: Vintage Books, 1996), p. 21.

3. Bruce Hampton, *The Great American Wolf* (New York: Henry Holt and Company, Inc., 1997), p. 16.

4. Ibid., p. 16.

5. Ibid., p. 25.

6. *Canis rufus,* The IUCN Red List of Threatened Species, Species Information, 2004, <http://www.redlist.org/search/details.php?species=3747> (October 25, 2005).

7. Rick McIntyre, ed., *War Against the Wolf: America's Campaign to Exterminate the Wolf* (Stillwater, Minn.: Voyageur Press, 1995), p. 33.

8. Steinhart, p. 164.

9. Mech, p. 25.

10. U.S. Fish and Wildlife Service, "Red Wolf Recovery/Species Survival Plan," October 1990, p. 6, <http://ecos.fws.gov/species_profile/servlet/gov.doi.species_profile.servlets.SpeciesProfile?> (May 17, 2006).

11. *Canis rufus,* The IUCN Red List of Threatened Species, p. 5.

12. *Canis rufus,* The IUCN Red List of Threatened Species, p. 2.

Chapter 2. A Wolf's Life

1. U.S. Fish and Wildlife Service, "Red Wolf News," vol. 5, issue 2, Summer, 2004.

2. U.S. Fish and Wildlife Service, "Red Wolves," *Sewee Visitor and Environmental Education Center,* n.d., <http://www.fws.gov/seweecenter/red_wolf_infor_.htm> (December 22, 2005).

3. U.S. Fish and Wildlife Service, "Red Wolf News," vol. 5, issue 2, Summer, 2004.

4. Barry Holstun Lopez, *Of Wolves and Men* (New York: Charles Scribner's Sons, 1978), p. 33.

5. L. David Mech, *The Wolf: The Ecology and Behavior of an Endangered Species* (Minneapolis: University of Minnesota Press, 1970), p. 4.

6. Ibid., p. 134.

7. Ibid., pp. 138–139.

8. Lopez, p. 37.

9. Mech, p. 89.

10. Kim Long, *Wolves: A Wildlife Handbook* (Boulder, Colo.: Johnson Books, 1996), p. 76.

11. Lopez, p. 43.

12. Long, p. 70.

13. Mech, p. 98.

14. Ibid., p. 99.

15. Ibid., p. 108.

16. Alligator River National Wildlife Refuge Red Wolf Program, "Top Ten Frequently Asked Questions About Red Wolves," p. 4, n.d., <http://www.outer-banks.com/alligator-river/redwolf.asp> (December 9, 2005).

17. Michael Morse, "Red Wolves of Alligator River: Bluestone Pack Forms," *Field Trip Earth,* n.d., <http://www.fieldtripearth.org/article.xml?id=1139> (October 27, 2005).

18. U.S. Fish and Wildlife Service, "Red Wolf News," vol. 5, issue 2, Summer, 2004.

Chapter 3. Threats

1. Rick McIntyre, ed., *War Against the Wolf: America's Campaign to Exterminate the Wolf* (Stillwater, Minn.: Voyageur Press, 1995), pp. 33–34.

2. Ibid., p. 51.

3. Bruce Hampton, *The Great American Wolf* (New York: Henry Holt and Company, Inc., 1997), p. 6.

4. McIntyre, p. 120.

5. Hampton, p. 132.

6. McIntyre, p. 199.

7. Jan DeBlieu, *Meant to Be Wild: The Struggle to Save Endangered Species Through Captive Breeding* (Golden, Colo.: Fulcrum Publishing, 1991), p. 31.

8. "Red Wolves," *Wildlife Science Center,* n.d., <http://www.wildlifesciencecenter.org/WolfRed.html> (January 16, 2006).

9. Hampton, p. 22.

10. L. David Mech, *The Wolf: The Ecology and Behavior of an Endangered Species* (Minneapolis: University of Minnesota Press, 1970), p. 322.

11. Colin Tudge, *Last Animals at the Zoo: How Mass Extinction Can Be Stopped* (Washington, D.C.: Island Press, 1992), p. 63.

12. Alligator River National Wildlife Refuge Red Wolf Program, "Top Ten Frequently Asked Questions About Red Wolves," n.d., p. 5, <http://www.outer-banks .com/alligator-river/redwolf.asp> (December 9, 2005).

13. *Canis rufus,* The IUCN Red List of Threatened Species, 2004, <http://www.redlist.org/search/ details.php?species=3747> (October 25, 2005).

14. U.S. Fish and Wildlife Service, "Red Wolf News," vol. 3, issue 1, July 2002, <www.fws.gov/ alligatorriver/rwnews/rwnews3-1.pdf> (December 15, 2005).

15. Hampton, p. 181.

16. Ibid., p. 182.

17. Bill Updike, "Wolf Song of the South," Defenders: *The Conservation Magazine of Defenders of Wildlife,* Spring 2005, <http://www.defenders.org/defendersmag/issues/ spring05/rdwolf.html> (December 8, 2005).

Chapter 4. Road to Recovery

1. Jan DeBlieu, *Meant to Be Wild: The Struggle to Save Endangered Species Through Captive Breeding* (Golden, Colo.: Fulcrum Publishing, 1991), pp. 31–32.

2. Bruce Hampton, *The Great American Wolf* (New York: Henry Holt and Company, Inc., 1997), p. 171.

3. Ibid., p. 175.

4. U.S. Fish and Wildlife Service, "Red Wolf Recovery/Species Survival Plan," October 1990, p. 9, <http://ecos.fws.gov/species_profile/servlet/gov.doi .species_profile.servlets.SpeciesProfile?> (May 18, 2006).

5. DeBlieu, p. 46.

6. Ibid., p. 41.

7. U.S. Fish and Wildlife Service, "Red Wolf Recovery/Species Survival Plan," p. 11.

8. Ibid.

9. Peter Steinhart, *The Company of Wolves* (New York: Vintage Books, 1996), p. 171.

10. DeBlieu, p. 42.

11. Ibid., p. 48.

12. Ibid.

13. U.S. Fish and Wildlife Service, "Red Wolf Recovery/Species Survival Plan," p. 12.

Chapter 5. Wild Again

1. U.S. Fish and Wildlife Service, "Red Wolf Recovery/Species Survival Plan," October 1990, p. 13, <http://ecos.fws.gov/species_profile/servlet/gov.doi .species_profile.servlets.SpeciesProfile?> (May 18, 2006).

2. Peter Steinhart, *The Company of Wolves* (New York: Vintage Books, 1996), pp. 172–173.

3. U.S. Fish and Wildlife Service, "Red Wolf Recovery/Species Survival Plan," p. 13.

4. Bruce Hampton, *The Great American Wolf* (New York: Henry Holt and Company, Inc., 1997), p. 180.

5. Steinhart, p. 174.

6. U.S. Fish and Wildlife Service, Federal Register,

"Endangered and Threatened Wildlife and Plants;
Determination of Experimental Population Status for an
Introduced Population of Red Wolves in North Carolina,"
vol. 51, no. 223, p. 41792.

7. Jan DeBlieu, *Meant to Be Wild: The Struggle to
Save Endangered Species Through Captive Breeding*
(Golden, Colo.: Fulcrum Publishing, 1991), pp. 18–19.

8. Ibid., p. 24.

9. Ibid., p. 69.

10. Ibid., p. 75.

11. Ibid., p. 82.

12. U.S. Fish and Wildlife Service, "Red Wolf
Recovery/Species Survival Plan," p. 17.

13. *International Wolf* magazine, "Red Wolf
Restoration Halted in Great Smoky Mountains National
Park," Spring 1999, <http://www.wolf.org/wolves/
learn/intermed/inter_red/red_restoration_smoky.asp>
(January 27, 2006).

14. U.S. Fish and Wildlife Service, "Red Wolf
Recovery/Species Survival Plan," pp. 18–19.

15. *International Wolf* magazine, "Red Wolf
Restoration Halted in Great Smoky Mountains National
Park," Spring 1999.

16. "Historic Timeline for the Endangered Red
Wolf," *The Red Wolf Coalition,* n.d., <http://www
.redwolves.com/about_recovery/timeline.html>
(December 8, 2005).

Chapter 6. Captive Breeding

1. "Zoo Asks for Breeding Program Donations,"
International Wolf Center, July 7, 2004, <http://
www.wolf.org/wolves/news/live_news_detail.asp?id=
146> (January 12, 2006).

2. "Species Survival Plan Program," *The American
Zoo and Aquarium Association,* n.d., <http://www.aza
.org/ConScience/ConScienceSSPFact/> (November 21,
2005).

3. *Canis rufus,* The IUCN Red List of Threatened Species, 2004, <http://www.redlist.org/search/details.php ?species=3747> (October 25, 2005).

4. Author interview with Will Waddell, Coordinator of the RWSSP Captive Breeding Program, Point Defiance Zoo, January 28, 2006.

5. U.S. Fish and Wildlife Service, "Red Wolf Recovery/Species Survival Plan," October 1990, p. 17, <http://ecos.fws.gov/species_profile/servlet/gov.doi .species_profile.servlets.SpeciesProfile?> (May 18, 2006).

6. E-mail interview with Kim Scott, Assistant Director, Wild Canid Survival and Research Center, January 24, 2006.

7. U.S. Fish and Wildlife Service, "Red Wolf Recovery/Species Survival Plan," p. 17.

8. U.S. Fish and Wildlife Service, "Temporary Closure of the Bulls Island Red Wolf Propagation Project," December 2005, <http://www.fws.giv/caperomain/ RWClosure.htm> (December 22, 2005).

9. "Historic Timeline for the Endangered Red Wolf," *The Red Wolf Coalition,* n.d., <http://www.redwolves .com/about_recovery/timeline.html> (December 8, 2005).

10. The Conservation Breeding Specialist Group (SSC/IUCN) and the United States Fish and Wildlife Service, "Red Wolf *(Canis rufus)* Population and Habitat Viability Assessment (PHVA) Workshop Report," Virginia Beach, Virginia, April 13–16, 1999.

11. Ibid., p. 4.

12. Ibid., p. 12.

Chapter 7. An Uncertain Future

1. U.S. Fish and Wildlife Service, Division of Endangered Species, Red Wolf, Species Accounts, *Canis rufus,* n.d., <http://www.fws.gov/Endangered/i/a/ saa04.html> (May 18, 2006).

2. *Canis rufus,* The IUCN Red List of Threatened Species, 2004, <http://www.redlist.org/search/details .php?species=3747> (October 25, 2005).

3. Shauna Baron, USFWS Red Wolf Recovery Program, "Red Wolf Fostering Is a Success," U.S. Fish and Wildlife Service, December 20, 2002, <http:// news.fws.gov/NewsReleases/showNews.cfm?newsID= 295D4757-2435-4FF1-A3D> (December 12, 2005).

4. U.S. Fish and Wildlife Service, "Red Wolf News," vol. 5, issue 2, Summer, 2004.

5. Dr. Gail Y. B. Lash and Pamela Black, Ursa International, "Red Wolves: Creating Economic Opportunity Through Ecotourism in Rural North Carolina," Report (Washington, D.C.: Defenders of Wildlife, February 2005).

Grambo, Rebecca L. *Wolf: Legend, Enemy, Icon.* Richmond, Ont.: Firefly Books, 2005.

Gunzi, Christiane. *The Best Book of Wolves and Wild Dogs.* New York: Kingfisher, 2003.

Landau, Diana, ed. *Wolf: Spirit of the Wild: A Celebration of Wolves in Word and Image.* New York: Sterling Publishing Company, Inc., 2000.

Leach, Michael. *Wolf: Habitats, Life Cycles, Food Chains, Threats.* Austin, Tex.: Raintree Steck-Vaughn, 2003.

Markle, Sandra. *Wolves.* Minneapolis: Carolrhoda Books, 2004.

Patent, Dorothy Hinshaw. *Back to the Wild.* San Diego: Harcourt Brace, 1997.

Rogers, Lesley J., and Gisela Kaplan. *Spirit of the Wild Dog: The World of Wolves, Coyotes, Foxes, Jackals, and Dingoes.* Crows Nest, N.S.W., Australia: Allen and Unwin, 2003.

Thiel, Richard P. *Keeper of the Wolves: The Early Years of Wolf Recovery in Wisconsin.* Madison: University of Wisconsin Press, 2001.